Praise for *Overcoming Chronic Disorganization*

'A must have for everyone working with or challenged by disorganization.'

James Wallman, bestselling author, keynote speaker,
cultural commentator

'If you have issues with chronic disorganization or hoarding, this book will help you understand why; and it offers clear, practical solutions to do something about it.'

Emma Corcoran, client

'Jo Cooke takes a transdiagnostic approach to the problem of chronic disorganization, which can be present with a number of mental health conditions and beyond. This book will be valuable for anyone with neurodiversity and hoarding disorder. Jo Cooke's two editions on hoarding problems have proved to be a valuable contribution to the resources for both people with the problem and those who work professionally with them. This book is certain to do the same for people with chronic disorganization.'

Dr Stuart Whomsley, co-author, 'A Psychological
Perspective on Hoarding'

'Jo offers us here a comprehensive and accessible view of the range of complexities that lead to full and overwhelming home environments, and super strategies to help find an area we can control. But she does this with great humanity and empathy, and with hope, and that makes this a terrific and essential read for anyone facing challenges with their routines and belongings.'

Jasmine Sleigh, author of *Being Owned: A Decade in
Professional Decluttering*, and owner of Change Your Space

T0271790

'Jo explains what chronic disorganization is in an easy to read, compassionate, and empathetic way. Sharing her own experiences and that of others, Jo breaks down the different ways chronic disorganization presents itself. Her use of stories of clients and her own experiences as well as quoting other references provides variety and an ability for the reader to connect with the topic. For anyone who wants to understand more about chronic disorganization, start here!'

Siân Pelleschi, president, APDO, and founder, Sorted!

Overcoming Chronic Disorganization

Also by Jo Cooke

Understanding Hoarding: Reclaim Your Space and Your Life

On related topics, from Sheldon Press

Overcoming Procrastination, Windy Dryden

Autism in Adults, Dr Luke Beardon

Managing Anxiety in Autistic Adults, Dr Luke Beardon

About the author

Jo Cooke is the Director of Hoarding Disorders UK and an accredited member of the Association of Professional Declutterers and Organisers (APDO). She is also an international trainer on delivering hoarding training. Her previous career included working for charitable organizations, human resources, project management, book-keeping and civil service, amongst others.

Overcoming Common Problems

Overcoming Chronic Disorganization
Finding Strategies That Work

JO COOKE

First published in Great Britain by Sheldon Press in 2024
An imprint of John Murray Press

5

Copyright © Jo Cooke 2024

A CIP catalogue record for this title is available from the British Library

Trade Paperback ISBN 978 1 399 81336 5
ebook ISBN 978 1 399 81337 2

Typeset by KnowledgeWorks Global Ltd.

Printed and bound in Great Britain by Clays Ltd, Elcograf S.p.A.

John Murray Press policy is to use papers that are natural, renewable and recyclable products and made from wood grown in sustainable forests. The logging and manufacturing processes are expected to conform to the environmental regulations of the country of origin.

John Murray Press
Carmelite House
50 Victoria Embankment
London EC4Y 0DZ

www.sheldonpress.co.uk

John Murray Press, part of Hodder & Stoughton Limited
An Hachette UK company

The authorised representative in the EEA is Hachette Ireland, 8 Castlecourt Centre, Dublin 15, D15 XTP3, Ireland (email: info@hbgi.ie)

To Wilf

Contents

Introduction

Since I wrote my book *Understanding Hoarding* in 2017, I have learned so much. I have learned that we can all be impacted by having too much stuff and living in congested homes, leaving many of us with a complete sense of overwhelm. It could be because we have difficulty letting go of items and of the associated memories, but it may also be that this has not been our priority given the other challenges we are faced with in navigating the demands of modern life.

The COVID-19 pandemic gave us all time to reflect about how our homes work for us, and for some it was the ideal opportunity to tackle those 'I'll do it when I have time' jobs. Lockdown gave us the perfect opportunity to focus on issues that we would otherwise have put aside. However, for some of us, lockdown provided the opposite – a sense of inertia and a licence to 'lapse'.

I have also come to realize that, in the dozens of homes I have worked in over the last ten years, there is a certain blindness to the mess within the physical environment that, in turn, is often a reflection of my clients' emotional environment. For some clients it suddenly reaches a crisis point when they are unable to find their passport and consequently miss a holiday, or they miss a special dinner because they can't find their car keys, or miss a concert because they have mislaid their tickets.

Sometimes we have to reach a crisis point many times over before we recognize that we need help and accept that asking for help is a sign of wisdom, not weakness.

I have also learned that the tides and landscape of our homes can often change and present differently depending on our mood, our energy and what is happening in our lives – whether it be biological, situational or the fact that a life event is increasing the sense of anxiety and stress that consumes us. This can result in our not being able to find things, put things away, pay bills on time, keep appointments, and so on. In turn, this leads to a cluttered, chaotic and confused environment.

There is a common belief that clutter is a manifestation of our mind, our mood and our motivation, but that it may also be associated with hoarding behaviours. We talk about needing to delve deeper, with curiosity, compassion and conversations to find the meaning in the mess. We are complicated human beings and our relationship with our environment and how we manage it is complex.

Throughout this book, clients' names have been changed to protect their identity in the stories told.

1
What is chronic disorganization?

You may wonder why we talk about 'chronic disorganization' rather than just 'disorganization'. Chronic disorganization is disorganization that occurs over a number of years, may well show up in the teen years, and can significantly undermine one's quality of life on a daily basis.

For the purposes of ease, chronic disorganization will be abbreviated and referred to as CD.

> **Did you know?**
>
> There is an Institute for Challenging Organization (ICD) based in the USA. The organization has very valuable resources. https://www.challengingdisorganization.org/

Author Judith Kolberg, who wrote *Conquering Chronic Disorganization*, first coined the phrase 'chronic disorganization' in 1992 and defined it as having three main features:

- the persistence of severe disorganization over a long period of time
- the daily undermining of one's quality of life by disorganization
- a history of failed self-help attempts.

Some of its common manifestations include:

- cluttered living areas
- missing important documents
- habitual lateness due to misplaced items or distractions
- difficulty completing tasks such as laundry
- multiple projects begun but not finished
- poor sense of time

- difficulty making decisions
- missing deadlines
- inability to find things – gloves, earphones and phone chargers are common items
- forgetting to take and/or running out of medication
- running out of toilet rolls
- paying penalties for unpaid bills, late tax returns and speeding fines
- missing doctors/hospital/dental appointments.

For some, CD may well impact on their ability to hold down a job, complete a degree, maintain friendships and hold a family together, as well as leaving a dent in their self-esteem. Feelings of uselessness and a lack of self-worth can impact on wellbeing.

I hear so often, too, from clients who say they are functioning well in their work life but, when it comes to managing their homes, they just can't do it. I work with many clients who have highly successful careers, but their homes are in chaos. Some can focus their energies only on one area of their lives – addressing the functioning of a home is not a priority.

Our emotional tank often needs refuelling to be able to address avoidance areas in our lives. There is the often heard phrase: 'I've got nothing left in the tank.' Often, we avoid tasks because they may feel mundane, tedious and challenging. We need to look at what avoidance is about, and also how best to use our energies.

Cluttered living areas

You may know someone who is affected by the following – or perhaps these things resonate for you?

- clothes not stored away
- piles of stuff in random places
- bags of shopping not put away
- unopened post in various places
- recycling overflowing
- floor space filled with a plethora of items
- items identified for charity still not at their destination
- items identified as rubbish still not in the bin

- bins overflowing
- luggage not unpacked following a trip away
- vouchers expiring
- cheques uncashed
- currency not exchanged
- washing up not completed and stacking up by the sink
- items that have been bought and found not suitable still waiting to be returned
- the buying of gifts and cards not appropriate to the occasion they are intended for – for example a birthday card bought for a christening.

There is often, too, an overspill of items into inappropriate rooms or places. One of my clients used her unused dishwasher to store her receipts. Another person I know uses her bedroom to store excess food tins that she bought during lockdown. Often, people's cars, too, can become as cluttered, disordered and as messy as their homes.

No (or multiple) systems in use

I often see ineffectual attempts at organization which involve the acquisition of, for example, bulldog clips. I worked with one woman who needed to separate out like-for-like paperwork and, as we didn't have any folders but I did have a clutch of bulldog clips, we used these to separate gas bills from credit card bills and so on. When I went back to see her a month later, she had bought more bulldog clips, but was not actually using them. (Some people might not use the bulldog clips until they have all different sizes, shapes and colours.)

Sometimes, the tops of piles become the system we use to be able to remember and action things, so we keep them in prominent places. If anyone comes into the house and starts to move items – perhaps because they're worried that a pile of paperwork is about to take a tumble! – this can be hugely distressing and disorienting for someone who is chronically disorganized. Now they have to try to work out where items may have been relocated to – another source of stress. Such items can include:

- box files
- storage boxes/containers of various sizes
- diaries
- sticky notes
- calendars
- shoe storage systems
- various clocks and alarm systems
- gadgets that help you find keys
- numerous remote controls
- to-do notebooks
- magnetic to-do lists
- books on how to get organized!

Some people have no systems in place, and they might heavily rely on knowing exactly where they left it to be able to retrieve it. This, combined with other people moving things around, can be disastrous.

The intention to become organized is often there, but the implementation of a system is – or seems – beyond reach and is not maintained. Organizing is a process rather than an event, and for many the ongoing maintenance of being organized can be challenging. I like to compare this to the way in which some people try to lose weight: though they recognize that they need to keep up the hard work to carry on losing that weight, they find it difficult to keep to the diet plan and the weight creeps back on, in just the same way as clutter and disorganization can take hold again. Gardening makes another good comparison: If you don't do regular maintenance, ivy has a way of creeping back and weeds will ruthlessly reappear.

Mislaid important documents

These include:

- passport
- birth certificate
- marriage certificate
- driving licence
- insurance documents
- council tax notification
- National Insurance (NI) number
- National Health Service (NHS) number
- children's health records
- P60 and other employment-related documents
- vaccination documents
- degree certificate(s)
- examination certificate(s).

Did you know?

Replacement birth, death, marriage and civil partnership certificates can be ordered on line via the General Register Office in England. Title deeds to properties can also be ordered via the Land Registry.

Lateness due to misplaced items or distractions

Have you missed an appointment – perhaps an eye examination, a doctor's appointment or a parent's evening – because you cannot find your car keys? I for one remember my mum taking me back to boarding school on the wrong day. I was devastated. Or perhaps we become distracted because we are enjoying ourselves swimming in the sea and then completely forget we have an appointment with the asthma nurse. Lateness for me can seem as if the late person doesn't care about you enough to turn up on time. Others intentionally turn up late because they are angry with someone – it can be passive aggressive – or because they feel self-entitled – they are just too important to turn up on time!

Time blindness and lateness and tactics to deal with them are covered later in this chapter. I think having awareness of your behaviours and the various causes behind them means that you can then work on them.

Difficulty completing daily tasks

Laundry is a lifetime activity, and it never ends. You may have a moment of sheer bliss at the thought of being on top of your laundry, with everything clean and ironed and neatly put away, but then you remember that, by the end of the day, you will have created more dirty laundry. The cycle of laundry is endless and for many it's overwhelming.

Did you know?

The term 'floordrobe' is used to describe an untidy pile of clothes that have been left on the floor. Similarly, we might also have the 'chairdrobe' which acts as transit storage. The clothes are not yet dirty enough to put in the laundry basket, but not clean enough to put away. They also make an easy grab when you need something to put on quickly.

The laundry conundrum

Gail is 65 years old and an illustrator. She has hoarding tendencies, is chronically disorganized and has compulsive acquisition behaviours.

She suffers from depression, and her CD can lead to her being unable to work for months on end. Her husband thinks she has undiagnosed attention deficit hyperactivity disorder (ADHD), but her lack of organization has meant that as yet she has been unable to fill in the details and forms for the diagnosis!

The main triggers for her hoarding behaviours were initially abandonment issues related to childhood and later empty nest syndrome when her grown-up children left home in their mid-twenties. Her compulsive acquisition kicks in when she has money, leading her to shop online and trawl through charity shops. In an attempt to defuse any criticism from her husband, she buys a lot of items for other people.

She is a non-finisher so when making breakfast she will leave the milk out on the side with the top off, along with the bread for making toast. The used teabag will be left on the kitchen counter, and the lid from the butter dish will be left open with a used knife lying across it.

One of her biggest challenges is laundry. She doesn't have a laundry basket, so any dirty clothes are left on the kitchen floor in front of the washing machine. They can be there for days.

When they eventually make it into the washing machine, after the wash, three things may happen:

They are washed and hung up on the wooden rail above the sliding door into the garden. (She doesn't have a tumble dryer.)

They are washed and left in the washing machine until they begin to smell and must be washed again.

They are pulled out of the washing machine and left on the floor until she remembers to hang them up to dry. Sometimes they need to be washed again as they have been left for too long.

The clothes are usually left to dry for days, well beyond the required drying time. From there, Gail eventually moves them to the lounge where they are placed on the back of a chair, waiting to be ironed. There they can stay for days and sometimes weeks. Finally when they do get ironed, they can stay in a pile on the stairs for a few days before being taken upstairs and put away. Sometimes Gail gets distracted and puts them on her bed. Occasionally, they stay on the bed overnight and get kicked off and must be folded or ironed again.

The laundry process is never done in a day. The average laundering time for an item of clothing is around one week but sometimes it may take over a month.

After discussion with me, the couple concluded that, as Gail's husband is fairly organized and practical, he should take on the task of doing the laundry, using more laundry baskets to identify the dirty from the clean, and making sure that the clothes, once cleaned, dried and ironed, are put swiftly away.

I know for many it is simply easier to buy new clothes or clothes from charity shops than it is to tackle the laundry. I once jokingly told someone that having disposable clothes was a solution to their disorganization regarding the laundry.

It is also important to address the fact that, for some people, being clueless about how to use a washing machine is a real thing. There is a famous actor who once posted on Instagram asking where the washing powder was meant to be inserted. People can be bamboozled by what cycle to use, how to separate items into colours and whites, the symbols on the labels of clothing, or how many items can be considered a load or a half load. What constitutes a woollen wash, a quick wash, an eco-wash? What do you put in a gentle cycle wash? For someone who has not been shown all this, the washing machine can present a huge challenge.

A client who lived with his father for some of his childhood was often fed up with the fact that he hardly ever seemed to have a clean school uniform, or if it was clean, it had been forgotten about and not put in the dryer. His response to growing up in that environment is that, as soon as he identifies there's sufficient dirty laundry to constitute a load, the load goes on. The first thing he did as part of independent living skills when he went to university was to have someone show him how to use the hall of residence washing machine and dryer.

Doing laundry can be grounding, but laundry is the real never-ending story.

Multiple projects/tasks begun but not finished

Sometimes projects are not finished because interest dwindles, inspiration fails, or life becomes too busy. For some people a project may grow tedious, not provide stimulation, or prove too difficult. There can be a lack of focus or sometimes a paralysing tendency to hyperfocus or overfocus (see box). This is especially true for someone with ADHD who requires the right amount of dopamine for the brain to go into the right gear to carry on with the project to the end. Completing a project for someone with ADHD can feel like swimming against a strong current or wading through mud. I have read that incomplete projects are like abandoned ships – and, in many cases, there can be a whole fleet of ships!

Kinds of focus

Hyperfocus

If a project or task is really stimulating and appealing, we can lose complete track of time and space and be wholly absorbed in the project for hours, although to us it may seem like only a short time. Time whizzes past and nothing feels tedious or arduous. It is the complete opposite to swimming against the tide – the swim is self-propelling. This is called hyperfocus and can be a symptom of someone with ADHD, in whom it needs to be celebrated as a strength.

My friend Cherry has a diagnosis of ADHD. When Cherry and I, together with another friend, Heather, were planning on travelling to a conference on hoarding in San Francisco, we gave Cherry the task of researching the best hotel and flights – we knew that research is a real strength for Cherry. In fact, if there is any type of research needed, I ask Cherry. Her middle name is, we fondly say, 'Research'.

Hyperfocus can be a challenge or a superpower regardless of whether you have ADHD or not or are neurotypical or neurodivergent. The need to recognize when hyperfocusing can lead to obsessive activity is something to be aware of. It is important to understand/identify when hyperfocusing on something has a positive outcome which can lead to a decision or action as opposed to hyperfocusing on something that leads to paralysis and therefore causing needs to not being met.

Overfocus

I find that this tends to occur as a trait in clients who may exhibit obsessive-compulsive behaviours and/or personalities. Overfocus can lead to a paralysis of inactivity as the need to have the project or task perfect can often be to the detriment of the task even before it has started (see the discussion on perfectionism in Chapter 2). A fear of danger, constant negative thoughts and high levels of anxiety are experienced. Repetitive thoughts sit alongside the over-focus, and with them come stubbornness and rigidity. In contrast to hyperfocus, overfocus tends to have more negative connotations and is more connected with obsessive compulsive disorder (OCD) and obsessive compulsive personality disorder (OCPD) rather than ADHD. As with all behaviours and personality traits, it does not necessarily come with a label or diagnosis.

Hypofocus

This is the opposite of hyperfocus – *hypo* means 'deficient'. Again, this is something I see in many clients in terms of the inability to con-centrate, or only in a limited way, on completing a task or project.

Wine bottles, roll-on deodorants and wadges of wool

I have worked with two male clients who are both, incidentally, engineers and who both have, to me – as a neurotypical person – quite an exhausting, albeit methodical, way of recycling. My way of recycling a bottle of wine is to put the bottle in the glass recy-cling and the screw cap, if there's not a cork, in the metal recycling. One of the men needed to extract the foil of the neck of the bottle and also steam the paper off. We had several conversations about how this could be done differently but he was rigid in his think-ing and dubious as to what happened to the bottles once they reached the recycling unit.

Another man had the same thinking concerning roll-on deo-dorants. He felt the need to extract the rollerball – which is glass – from the deodorant stick before recycling. He probably had over fifty deodorant sticks ready to prepare for recycling, but the task had become so arduous that he never got round to it.

I worked with one woman (who has sadly subsequently died) whose mission was to achieve 'a tidy death'. She had no family, and I was involved with sorting through her items. The items I removed filled a third of my garage: unfinished knitting projects – from baby cardigans, to shawls, blankets and hats. She would start a project but did not have the focus to finish it. My local knitting group took away the wool and the woollen projects and finished them off. They sent me photographs of the finished projects and they were donated to the Air Ambulance Service, a charity my client supported. We look at CD in end-of-life contexts more closely in Chapter 10.

Time blindness

This can also be described as a poor sense of time, which we will look at more closely in Chapter 4 along with tips for managing time better. Time blindness can imply that you overestimate or underestimate how long a task will take to complete, though typically my clients underestimate the size and scale of a task. It can also mean that many people overcommit on engagements, projects and meetings, with a propensity to try to jam so much in that they eventually become overloaded and burn out.

For many, too, time blindness can mean that they always try to cram in one last thing before they leave, with the result that they are always late for an appointment. If you are anxious, and renowned for always being late, it may result in you being super early instead. Factoring in distractions and predicting how long something will take is often challenging, and time may not be well planned out.

The implications of tardiness are huge, in terms of feeling that we cannot meet deadlines, miss appointments and are generally perceived as unreliable. This can often lead to our feeling frustrated and judged.

In his book *Indistractable: How to Control Your Attention and Choose Your Life*, Nir Eyal puts it neatly: 'Time management is pain management.'[1] For those who have a structure, routine and

---

[1] Nir Eyal, with Julie Li, *Indistractable: How to Control Your Attention and Choose Your Life* (BenBella Books, 2019), p. 27 (Chapter 4 is devoted to the topic).

schedule to follow, time is that much easier to manage as they become accustomed to the rhythm and repetition of their daily lives. For others, time management can be a continual challenge, especially if they have early morning commitments.

We all have 24 hours in a day. James Wallman, author of *Stuffocation* and *Time and How to Spend It*, suggests that there are seven reasons why we feel time poor. These importantly include:

- We think busyness has status
- Instead of helping, multitasking creates 'contaminated time' – that is, scrolling through our phone while at the park with our children
- Smartphones and all our digital devices now eat up 60 per cent of our leisure time.

Difficulty making decisions

This can also link with making poor choices, and I have worked with many clients who really struggle with making decisions over what to eat for lunch, what clothes to wear, what car to buy as well as general prioritizing. So much of our decision making involves the unrelenting perfectionism that invariably leads to paralysis through fear of making the wrong decision (we will cover perfectionism in another chapter). Many clients berate themselves over poor choices or the fact that they are stuck in a decision-making limbo.

It is not surprising we have difficulty making decisions. Going to a supermarket to buy teabags, we are met with so much choice. Do we buy decaffeinated, fairtrade, organic, English tea, Darjeeling, a luxury brand, Christmas tea, herbal tea, tea to make us relax, to energize us …? Then we have a further decision to make – do I buy the supermarket's own brand, or the household brand, the value or the expensive option? We may also wonder why one brand might be cheaper than the other, and whether buying the most expensive means the best.

I painted my spare bedroom white recently. I was sure what shade of white I wanted – I didn't want anything too clinical or 'cold'. I looked at a colour swatch and spent many hours researching which shade of white worked best given the position of the sun and the amount of light. South, west, east and north facing ... I was faced with twelve different shades of white! After weeks of deliberation and consultation with friends I ended up with School House White. Now the bedroom actually does feel like a Victorian classroom and doesn't even look white – more pale green! Ugh!

Interestingly, the supermarkets that are prospering nowadays are those that offer less choice, not more. I also think the same can be said of restaurants and their menus. I remember as a child being in Greece on holiday and poring through huge plastic folders with pictures of the various dishes on offer – steak and chips, fish and chips, moussaka and chips, lambchops and chips. I understand the menus were presented in this way for an international, non-Greek-speaking audience, but the time it took to decide, given the bewildering choice, was endless. Inevitably, I would choose the 'special'. Now the restaurants that work best for me are those with short, carefully crafted menus, with just three or four choices per course.

Choice overload

A great deal is written about this and how we can become completely overwhelmed by the array of choices and decisions that we are presented with – from buying teabags to making key life changes. We can become paralysed by this. I know that when my father considered moving from the family home I grew up in, he found the decisions he had to make about the type of house he might want to live in, together with its location and cost, so onerous that he ended up not moving at all.

I know I have certain clothes that I wear for work, for training, for cleaning, for evenings out – this helps me make choices quickly and without too much fuss. Work uniforms are often popular with staff as it means that there are no decisions to be made. Monday–Sunday underwear is popular for the same reason. There are choices and decisions to make not just about what we eat, wear, what coffee to order, what moisturizer to buy, but also what doctor or dentist to visit, what dating website to subscribe to, what pronoun to use, what course to take, what channel to watch.

In his book *The Paradox of Choice*, Barry Schwartz writes about the explosion of choice in the contemporary Western world – and how it doesn't necessarily give us freedom but anxiety, stress and depression. Instead of happiness, choice overload means we question our decisions before we make them, leading us to be critical of any poor decisions we eventually make. With that too comes 'analysis paralysis', which can lead to no decision being made at all – like my father not moving house. Schwartz explains how reducing our available choices can ease our stress and anxiety; he outlines some practical steps to show us how to cut them down to a more manageable number, helping us to prioritize those which matter most.

Decision fatigue, too, is very common as we become weary of the amount of choice offered because of modern technology and the pace of everyday life.

Did you know?

Decidophobia is the paralysing fear of making a wrong decision – any decision, whether it be everyday decisions or lifelong-impacting decisions.

Domestic 'black holes'

I use this expression because there are many black holes in the homes I work in. Sometimes, putting something away in a cupboard or in a box means that it is lost for ever. If we cannot see it, we forget it exists.

I have now come to realize that, if there are empty cupboards in a house I visit, it is generally not because that person is disinclined to put things away but more because they cannot rely on their working memory to remember that an item exists if they put it away. Wardrobes, too, may be empty because having clothes out in plain sight prompts them what to wear and not always wear the same thing.

Jim's spread

I worked with a man – I'll call him Jim – who spread *everything* out on view in his home, just in case he needed an item. Our first priority was to create a pathway to the bathroom and get the bathroom door to shut – currently blocked by his love for and abundance of car magazines. After all, if I was going to work with him, I would need comfort breaks and some privacy! As we decluttered and identified new homes for items, Jim came to recognize that he kept everything out in the open as a prompt: a reminder to shave, floss his teeth, take his medication.

I opened the cupboard under Jim's bathroom sink and saw it was empty. To me that gave joy as it equated to a storage solution. I gleefully put his pack of twelve toilet rolls in the cupboard and told my client that this was where they now lived. A month later I went back and there was another pack of toilet rolls on the bathroom floor. I felt disheartened but quickly understood that the purchase was not a hoarding/panic purchase (this was after the days of lockdown), but that he had simply forgotten that I had put them under the sink and purchased more as he thought he had run out. The expression 'out of sight, out of mind' is a relevant one here!

Object permanence

Did you know?

'Object permanence' is the ability to understand that an object continues to exist even though it can no longer be seen, heard or touched.

The Swiss child psychologist Jean Piaget (1896–1980) first coined the term 'object permanence' in 1963. He undertook investigations aimed at understanding at what age a child understood that people and things continued to exist even when they were out of sight. He hid a toy under a blanket and watched to see if the child searched for the hidden toy. His results found that children are around eight months old when they begin to search for the hidden toys, and concluded that it is at this age that we begin to form mental pictures of items in our minds.

I believe that Piaget's idea can be applied to individuals with hoarding behaviours and/or neurological challenges such as ADHD, in that they may have an underdeveloped or diminished sense of object permanence. If an item is not in front of them, it does not exist. This could apply to people as much as to things. However, even if as adults we know in theory a relationship exists or an object exists, we do not necessarily hold this in our conscious mind. An example of this may be a passport that has been put away, or a phone that has been misplaced.

Shipshape

The word 'shipshape' is nautical in origin and refers to a sailor's need to keep their quarters neat, tidy and secure, not only because of the turbulence of being at sea but because of the confined space on board.

Interestingly, I know a couple of friends who have throughout their lives been impacted by CD, both in terms of their profession and home. However, both friends bought caravans and divulged to me that their caravans were kept orderly and tidy, in stark contrast to their homes (their description, not mine)!

Small spaces tend to be more defined in terms of their role, and items have to be kept carefully compartmentalized if the spaces are to work. Understanding how to utilize space and having an inventory of necessities can really help with the clutter we feel in our heads and therefore the physical clutter we have in our homes.

Five takeaways

1 Chronic disorganization (CD) is disorganization that occurs over a number of years, may well show up in the teen years, and can significantly undermine one's quality of life on a daily basis.
2 CD can affect every area of our life or sometimes just one area – our home but not our job, for example.

3 Typical manifestations include cluttered rooms, incomplete domestic tasks such as laundry, missed appointments or deadlines, and habitual mislaying of objects.

4 People with CD often have organization systems in place but are unable, for whatever reason, to see them through.

5 If we or someone we know is chronically disorganized, we can do something about it and help ourselves or them to lead better lives – read on!

2

Contributing factors and triggers

There are many contributing factors and triggers connected with chronic disorganization and we will cover many of them in this chapter. The reasons are varied and are often a combination of neurologically based causes, physical challenges, life crises, perfectionism, information-processing challenges, attachment to possessions and even factors such as poor storage space, motivation and procrastination. In Chapter 10, you will find a section on the relationship between growing older and CD.

Bereavement

Bereavement, grief and loss can affect us in many ways. Bereavement can take the form of any type of loss – a loss of a loved one, a marriage, a loss of a limb, a miscarriage, a job, a home, our possessions, a pet, or a life that was. The COVID-19 pandemic found many of us grieving a life we could not have or were denied. Grief is the price of love, and we are all affected by it in different ways and respond and behave uniquely.

There is no right and wrong way to grieve. Sometimes, it might be a song that triggers immense feelings of sadness, even many years after the loss. Our reactions to grief can be powerful. The emotions felt during mourning include paralysis, numbness, shock, sadness, anger, irritability and frustration. Feelings of overwhelm and immense tiredness and exhaustion can lead to inertia and feeling 'stuck'. We can feel as if we are losing our minds, and we feel fragile, vulnerable, depressed and anxious.

I remember when my mum died – one of my biggest and earliest losses – the thought of putting together a meal, creating an invoice, or having a shower took all of my energy and drained every ounce I felt I had left in my vessel. For some people who experience these feelings intensely, day-to-day living can be very challenging.

My divorce, too, led to poor decision making, rash and impulsive purchases, inability to concentrate and not being able to focus, all combined with forgetfulness. The impact bereavement has on those with hoarding behaviours is significant – they may not want to discard anything that belonged to the loved one because letting go of these seems to intensify the loss they are already experiencing.

Grief should not be underestimated. I know one local authority in the north of England that has acknowledged that there are many people with intense feelings of grief who are not coping well – so much so that it has begun a recruitment drive for bereavement counsellors.

Some of us take comfort in understanding the stages of grief. The Swiss-American psychologist Elizabeth Kübler-Ross (1926–2004) initially theorized the 'five stages of grief', though others have expanded the model to seven stages instead:

1 shock and disbelief
2 denial
3 guilt
4 anger and bargaining
5 depression, loneliness and reflection
6 reconstruction (or 'working through')
7 acceptance.

While there is a great deal of value in the model, we all grieve in our own way and may not necessarily experience all the stages in the order shown above or experience all of them at all. We can feel the rawness of mourning at any time and seemingly out of the blue. We need to accept that it is normal to feel the intensity of grief and not to push it away and feel that we should brush ourselves down and 'just get on with life'.

Sometimes grief lies unresolved for years or even decades. This sometimes gets linked to so-called 'complicated grief' (see box on the next page), or not feeling able to grieve or allowing yourself to feel your grief. Some of the signs for unresolved grief might include not wanting to speak about your loss, distracting yourself with busyness, seeking solace in too much food, exercise or drinking and wanting to sleep more. It may show up in an overreaction to another loss which might not be as relatively important, or in avoidance of close relationships for fear of being hurt.

Did you know?

Since 2022, grief is now a disorder that has an entry in *Diagnostic Statistical Manual, Fifth Edition* (*DSM-5*). It is also known as prolonged grief disorder. The disorder may sometimes be related to the way in which the person died – if it was sudden, early or violent, for example, without any opportunity to prepare for the loss – but there are also long-term predictors such as childhood separation anxiety and a close emotional dependency on the deceased.

Caroline's tides

Caroline was one of my first clients, and when we first started our sessions, she indicated that she needed someone to help her for the long haul. Initially, I was not sure what she meant but as the years passed, I learned why.

Caroline initially approached me for my help as an organizer/ declutterer shortly after the unexpected death of her husband. In response to her grief, she was struggling with many day-to-day challenges of running a home. Her husband had kept up with many of the household tasks such as dealing with paperwork, opening the post, paying the cleaner, having the chimneys swept, sending in tax returns on time, arranging trips to the vet, organizing holidays, making appointments for vaccinations, renewing passports, to name but a few. Their marriage was very much rooted in the acknowledgement and acceptance of the other partner's strengths, so there was a division of effort and this reinforced their strong partnership and shared goals.

After her husband's death Caroline had a dog, a rabbit, three children to care for while also coping with clouds of difficult emotions that included despair, depression, feelings of inadequacy, overwhelm and guilt, all steeped in deep grief in response to the loss of her husband.

Slowly, and at a pace that suited Caroline, we tackled the mountain of paperwork on the hall table, introduced a filing system that worked for Caroline, used colourful sticky notes to organize daily tasks that needed addressing, and adapted the household for a new norm.

I helped her move house and with that came a declutter. Caroline took great strength from her religious faith and had great resilience, but she also had a deep lack of confidence in her ability to maintain the home and all the challenges that came with that. It is probable that she has undiagnosed ADHD – she certainly recognizes how challenged she can be with finishing projects and how easily distracted she can be to stay on focus with mundane tasks. She is also not a naturally tidy person and has many different landing strips for when items come into her home. We have put strategies in place to overcome some of these issues, and some are still being honed.

There was a period during lockdown when I was not able to work with Caroline. However, with a lot of time, diminished distractions and a licence to focus that lockdown provided, Caroline was given time to reflect and facilitate other areas of her life that she wanted to enhance. This included organizing her diet and wellbeing. She bought a freezer and a slow cooker. She changed her diet, which to me was one of Caroline's biggest accomplishments as she had historically had a penchant for a certain burger drive-in. She effectively cleared her gut out.

Caroline maintained a diet of bone broth, fruits, green vegetables and plant-based foods. Improving Caroline's gut health has had a significant role in many areas of her physical and mental health and wellbeing. She has more energy, focus and concentration, has lost weight, has better sleep hygiene and increased motivation with reduced stress and improved mood. (We cover nutrition and diet in Chapter 3.)

I asked Caroline if she wanted to share any nuggets about what has helped her for this book, and she wanted to highlight that what has worked for her in overcoming chronic disorganization is having someone to help her stay focused, learning to put things away for easy retrieval and identifying homes for items. Putting things away means finding a logic for where that home might be, and so finding homes that are logical and easily accessible adds to efficient living rather than a daily struggle of recall and retrieval.

Caroline accepts that she is still challenged by establishing homes for miscellaneous items such as her picnic basket, lightbulbs, a guillotine cutter, her urns and Easter tree because there isn't an obvious place for them. She also shared the fact that she overthinks the question of how to dispose of items in her home – where to sell them, or who to donate them to. There's also the recycling – she worries whether an item can be recycled, whether the staff at the recycling unit will turn it away or whether the charity shop will accept its condition. In the face of such concerns, she confesses defeat.

I share all this because I do not want to offer a clear-cut before-and-after scenario but to stress that organization is an ongoing process – a realization of how acceptance of one's make-up, of one's strengths and weaknesses, and of learning to delegate and knowing how to ask for help can be liberating. Caroline is piecing together a functioning future.

Did you know?

'Hidy up' is a great expression that describes when someone tidies up in a hurry because visitors are expected home. Things are hidden away.

Perimenopause/menopause/post-menopause

Foggy, forgetful and flitty: these are the three words that best describe how I myself have been affected by menopause. There are many other symptoms that I could share, but not for the purposes of this book! I have come to accept that my brain works very differently now than it did ten years ago. I have to work very much harder at focusing on and completing jobs. Writing this book has been a lot harder than the *Understanding Hoarding* title I wrote seven years ago.

Menopause has affected the wiring of my brain, the organization (or disorganization, I should say) of my thoughts, and how my brain functions. Brain fog is a real thing – not just for those who are neurodivergent but for those going through any type of trauma, loss, grief and dementia. Brain fog for those going through menopause is due to an imbalance in hormones.

I forget names, and I forget words that I do not use frequently. I have written down a timeline of when events have happened in my life. I cannot multitask and find that, if I have a challenging task to confront, I have to block out so much more time and headspace to confront it.

Procrastination prevails so I now need a deadline to catapult me into action. I have had to acknowledge that this is my new norm. I have delegated tasks that challenge my concentration, and have embraced cold-water showers and open-water swimming as way of firing up my brain cells.

Many workplaces now recognize the impact that menopause can have on performance and make reasonable work adjustments for this. Hormone imbalance can contribute to the chaos in our functioning in the same way that poor diet, sleep, lack of exercise and medication do. Feelings of overwhelm and distractibility are also prevalent in those impacted by hormone imbalances.

ADHD impairment seems to peak in menopause according to a reader survey in ADHD consumer magazine *ADDitude*: 'Half of women surveyed called memory problems and overwhelm "life-altering" in their 40s and 50s, and 83% reported experiencing some ADHD symptoms for the first time in perimenopause and menopause.'[1]

Jo's muddle in menopause

My father had dementia, and I thought for a while I might have it, too. It can be scary thinking you might be 'losing your mind', but when you talk with other women you recognize that they too are challenged by the same issues. Some of us like a label of knowing what it is we have, to understand why we do what we do. I think also that I may well be affected by brain fog as a result of long-term stress and the effects of having had COVID-19.

I am managing my symptoms by trying to remember and cultivate good brain health habits that can provide protection of cognition and brain function. These include mindfulness, and my mindfulness includes any type of puzzle and a walk along the beach. Intellectual and physical activity help alongside good healthy eating habits, less alcohol and lots and lots of self-care. I feel so much better and focus more when I am hydrated, and always carry a water bottle with me. I relate and connect to other women experiencing the same difficulties, and that provides huge comfort. I swim in the sea as much as I can – I joke about the fact that it is not climate change making the sea warmer than it used to be, but the sheer amount of menopausal women swimming in it!

---

[1] 'ADHD impairment peaks in menopause, according to ADDitude reader survey', *ADDitude*, 5 June 2023, https://www.additudemag.com/menopause-symptoms-adhd-survey/

I am also aware how menopause has affected my self-esteem and confidence and am learning to adjust to new strategies to embrace these changes and not beat myself up. My best friend is a list: [having] a list of what to do each day and ticking things off my list is satisfying. There are days when I 'bring forward' my to-do list and that's fine. I exercise and have a good sleep routine. Days when I am more challenged than others – I turn off social media, am mindful of being mindless and recognize what steals my focus and attention. Cognitive function is something I am aware of and do as much as I can to maintain good brain health.

We discuss the usefulness of lists in Chapter 5.

Trauma

So many of our behaviours, our reactions and responses to our world are linked with trauma. One person's response to trauma can vary greatly from another's and how we cope in terms of day-to-day functioning and our sense of control. Trauma causes a disruption to our ability to cope with day-to-day living and can in turn lead chronic disorganization as we navigate the impact trauma can cause. Dr Gabor Maté has defined trauma as follows:

Trauma is a psychic wound that hardens you psychologically that then interferes with your ability to grow and develop. It pains you and now you're acting out of pain. It induces fear and now you're acting out of fear. Trauma is not what happens to you, it's what happens inside you as a result of what happened to you.[2]

When we think of trauma, we think of natural disasters, COVID-19, evacuation, sudden relocation, flooding, physical and sexual abuse, and catastrophe. But trauma can be less profound and less catastrophic and include any experiences that can debilitate us – including divorce, death, financial issues, incarceration, infidelity, legal issues and redundancy, to name but a few.

The literature suggests that there are little-'t' traumas and big-'T' traumas. One person may feel the trauma as a series of small traumas

---

[2] Dr Gabor Maté, in a YouTube interview, June 2019, https://www.youtube.com/watch?v=e7pV0IPWUlI

while others may experience trauma more profoundly. It is not necessarily connected with strength, being tough or made of steel when someone doesn't feel or remains unimpacted by trauma. The symptoms felt by trauma consist of an individual's distress tolerance, values, beliefs and, in some cases, expectations, morals and faith.

Any example of this includes our response to the COVID-19 lockdowns of 2020–21. For many, the effects of COVID-19 (which included anxiety, loneliness, uncertainly and isolation) led to unhealthy responses (e.g. excessive gaming, overeating/drinking, impulse purchases, neglect of oneself and surroundings), while others had a very different experience and were not necessarily so deeply impacted.

Some of us process experiences differently. Another example might be a soldier who has a diagnosis of post-traumatic stress disorder (PTSD) after combat, whereas another soldier in the same setting may not experience the same impact. The impact of a series of traumas and their accumulative effect should not be overlooked in terms of how it can affect a person's emotional wellbeing and functioning.

Adverse childhood experiences (ACEs)

ACEs are traumatic situations that occur during childhood. Research on ACEs details how trauma in childhood leaves an impression on our minds and bodies. They can impact on some-one's ability to manage their thoughts, emotions and feelings and often signal a threat to their safety and security.

Here are some of the identified ACEs:

- physical abuse
- sexual abuse
- emotional abuse
- living with someone who abused drugs
- living with someone who abused alcohol
- witnessing domestic violence
- living with someone who has gone to prison
- living with someone with serious mental illness
- losing a parent through divorce, death or abandonment.

Trauma can suppress parts of the brain, and – of interest to chronic disorganization – the prefrontal lobe can become suppressed – the part of the brain responsible for executive functioning.[3]

Sadie's acceptance of help

Sadie took part in some research in connection with ACEs, and she revealed to me that she had experienced many of them – including witnessing her mother's alcohol abuse and her eventual suicide, being threatened at knife point, surviving a hurricane and going through a divorce. Sadie has certainly had her fair share of tough times through-out her life and is not ashamed to share her experiences.

I have known Sadie for over thirty years, but it has probably only been in the last seven of these that I have come to know her past and worked with her to deal with her possessions, her environment, and her unopened post and offer strategies to help her not become so easily overwhelmed.

I interviewed her, and here I give her story in her own words:

Our whole flat was untidy. I lived with my mum, and Mum's bedroom was untidy. Mum was bipolar. I think they called it 'hypermania' in those days. She was also an alcoholic. My bedroom, too, was untidy, very much as it its now – piles on the floor in different categories.

My grandparents were ex-military and their home was immaculate. When I went to stay with them I never hesitated putting things away and clearing up. I remember the management and marshalling in their home. I loved the neatness and tidiness of their house and the routine and order and being told what to do. I never rebelled against them or it. I was a perfect grandchild.

My aunt (my mum's sister) lived in France, and her home was the same. I would stay with both my aunt and grandparents in the holidays. When I unpacked I would put things away, shoes lined up, suitcase put a way, flannel folded in the bathroom. I never deviated from this.

Later in my life when I had my own space, I reverted to the lunacy of mess. I then married – a man in the Forces who also liked neatness and order.

As a child, when I showed up for holidays at my grandparents, there would be a medley of clothes thrown into a suitcase. My grandparents took me clothes shopping every time and that involved buying shoes that fitted. They had to rebuild me every time.

---

[3] For more on ACEs, visit https://www.cdc.gov/violenceprevention/aces/index.html

During my school years I spent some time living with my best friend and then bought my first flat – I couldn't finish anything. I never finished decorating the dining room. I never had anyone over. The dining room became a dumping room. The dining room was utterly wasted.

My marriage broke down – my husband didn't talk; there was no communication. There was an incident in a helicopter where he was nearly killed. I suspect he had PTSD and was unhappy in our marriage.

After my divorce I moved and impulsively bought a home in Somerset. My aunt became ill and I spent three months in France. I cared for my aunt during this time. I had cared for my mother. My aunt died and then I had the challenge of sorting her home in France and also her home in Hampshire. I suddenly then had all the contents from France in my home in Somerset and from the house of another aunt in Somerset. I was also grieving. I became very overwhelmed.

I had a house in France to sort and sell, probate to sort. My performance at work was suffering and I was asked to leave. My aunt's house was left to me.

There's more on how Sadie dealt with – or is dealing with – her CD later in the chapter. Remember, it's always an ongoing project.

Trauma responses – fight, flight, freeze, fawn and flop

The sympathetic nervous system response originates to the earliest evolution of humans, when our ancestors came face to face with dangerous animals. The fight, flight, freeze, fawn or flop responses are how our body and mind respond to the threat of danger and to fear and uncertainty. They are survival instincts, and when there is a perception of danger our brain responds in these ways:

- **Fight** The fight response is when your body reacts to the threat of being attacked by, for example, a tiger. Your body automatically urges you to respond aggressively to the danger by fighting. This may mean that many people will stay in fight or combat mode for any other perceived threats that may emerge.
- **Flight** The flight response is when your body urges you to run away from the perceived threat of danger (e.g. the tiger). This is connected with and closely linked to avoidance. Many people in this mode may exercise excessively, be restless and feel tense and trapped.

- **Freeze** The freeze response is when you feel your body cannot fight or fly, and there is a hope that the tiger might just walk away. The body feels unable to act in response to danger. In some cases, this may be perceived as being 'stuck'.
- **Fawn** The fawn response is your body's emotional response to perceived danger when attempts of fight, flight or freeze have been unsuccessful. Signs include trying to appease the tiger. This response tends to occur with childhood trauma and signs include being overly helpful and agreeable as a means of soothing the perceived threat.
- **Flop** The flop response is when your body shuts down in response to coping with perceived danger and distress. It will play dead when it feels threatened by the tiger. Signs include disconnection, depression, anxiety and increased amount of sleep and apathy.

Autonomic nervous system (ANS)

Our autonomic nervous system is responsible for our body's response to threat and safety. Our nervous system can become dysregulated when we are impacted by trauma, anxiety and long-term stress.

Many people impacted by chronic disorganization and hoarding live in a state-of-survival mode – the fight-or-flight mode – when basic survival becomes a way of being and we fluctuate between the various modes as our nervous system becomes dysregulated.

There are many techniques you can apply to help soothe your nervous system including mindfulness, exercise, meditation, yoga, a healthy diet, technology-free time, singing, walking, cold-water plunges (this could be in the sea, a barrel or simply a few minutes of cold water in the shower) and walking on the beach, to name but a few.

I want to put a word in for smells, too. Studies have shown that certain aromas can suppress stress. There is a vast market and demand for essential oils and diffusers. My top tip is for when you find yourself steaming off wallpaper is to put a few drops of essential oils in the steamer. I particularly enjoy steaming wallpaper off with the smell of lemon grass or grapefruit in my airways!

Neuroplasticity

The good news, regarding CD, is that the way your brain is wired can change. Neuroplasticity can be defined as the ability of the brain to create new pathways to change and adapt the way it is wired, based on our experiences. Researchers have found that change can take place in the way the brain responds and reorganizes itself. Practices such as yoga and meditation help us focus and be aware of our 'default mode' and thereby help us towards changing that mode. Every new experience increases the potential for your brain to change. If we can change the way our brain works, we can embrace different ways of thinking and learn new ways of doing things, strengthen executive functioning and improve cognition.

There are various methods we can use to form new ways of thinking, for example:

- taking a new route to the shops
- learning a new language
- practising meditation
- taking regular naps

Moving house can have the same effect, though is perhaps not to be recommended on a frequent basis! All these practices can help us look at our world with fresh, more focused eyes and enable us to interact with it in a clearer, more purposeful way.

Sadie
We looked at Sadie's experience of CD earlier in the chapter. Here I want to share some of the questions I put to her during our interview, relating to how she is dealing with her condition.

1 Was there a point in your life that you decided that you wanted someone to come and work with you to declutter and/or organize?

After my aunts died I was overwhelmed with 'stuff' from multiple houses and a complicated legal mess. My best friend suggested (several times before I actually did it) that you would be a good person to help me.

2 What were the main benefits of having a professional organizer working with you?

An immediate relief that the problem was shared and now solvable. Practical steps to tackle what had seemed overwhelming on my own.

And someone to start me off with things. A sense of impetus and pur-pose. And gentle counselling.

3   What do you still find challenging in terms of organization and decluttering?

I am still inherently untidy and lazy. I leave my post and filing still. Putting things away – clean washing. Living alone does not help as there is no one to chivvy you up!

4   Do you have any nuggets that you can share in terms of staying on top of your environment, having a sense of wellbeing and feeling less overwhelmed?

I like my lists. I feel a sense of achievement as I tick things off. You taught me to also add 'nice' things to lists, not just drudgery. If you can afford it, get help. A cleaner will help keep you focused. Have a routine. Make your bed every day. Before you go to bed, wash up or load the dishwasher. Keep your kitchen under control and the rest will follow. Have set days for tasks – for example, change the bed on a Sunday.

I also reward myself for doing things – if I do the filing, I can buy a lipstick online etc. Shallow but it works for me. I also have to have nice smells. I burn incense and use a diffuser to make me calm. [The radio station] Classic FM also soothes me.

5   Is there an area of your home that you are dedicated to keeping tidy and organized?

I have a caravan which I keep neat and tidy. I recently had my bathroom renovated and it is my dream bathroom. It has stayed perfect. I like it being immaculate. My kitchen I love to clean each night before going to bed but my bedroom goes downhill easily.

6   What are areas of quick wins for you?

I like my sitting room to be neat. I can whizz round, put cushions in posi-tion, tidy the coffee table and relax.

And clean sheets and a tidy bed make me happy. [There's] [s]till crap round the edges of the bedroom but the bed will be neat.

7   I have one client who regularly cleans her fridge, and another who tidies her linen cupboard when they are feeling stressed. Once cleaned and tidied both clients feel a sense of relief, calm and control – is there anything you do to achieve the same?

I clean my bathroom. Particularly my mirrored cabinet. Has to be spar-kling and smear free and I am happy. Sometimes I clean it all and then I have a bath to relax, and then clean the bath again!

Sadie still loves expensive handbags, but struggles with buying good-quality washing powder. She thrives on a deadline but has actually done so many things on her to-do list that there is not much left. She has a will in place, has employed a cleaner, and has a routine of swimming and aerobics. When I visit she uses my presence and energy to complete some of the more arduous tasks that she has been putting off. We have addressed a lot of the clutter she has accumulated from her various relations' homes. Sadie was an only child and she recognizes that the stuff around her is comforting. She says that her hoard is her family and recognizes that her home is her nest, and perhaps the messiness of her bedroom is familiar, a constant. She suspects she has ADHD but sees it as a superpower.

Attention deficit hyperactivity disorder (ADHD)

There is a lot of media focus on what seems to be the increasing number of people being diagnosed with ADHD. I know that many of my CD clients believe they have ADHD but do not have a formal diagnosis. There is a kind of ADHD without the hyperactivity – attention deficit disorder (ADD). Many people with ADHD also have hoarding behaviours.

ADHD is defined as an individual having difficulty with:

- concentration
- attention
- hyperactivity
- impulsivity
- forgetfulness
- lateness
- emotional regulation
- planning
- following instructions
- organization.

I describe many of my clients as my butterflies – they flit from one interest or task to another and have difficulty staying on task and finishing the task to the end. The self-esteem of many people who do not have a diagnosis is low, and often they are very self-critical about how they struggle with day-to-day functioning and consider themselves stupid and lazy. Many of my clients have lost jobs because of their inability to perform, to keep on task, to keep to commitments and reach their performance goals.

Understanding how our brains are wired and how they work and thrive means that we can stop trying to put a round peg in a square hole and instead embrace our qualities and look for the strengths we have. One of my really positive clients claims that the upsides of having ADHD include having an abundance of energy and optimism. Some of the superpowers of having an ADHD brain are:

- ability to research any given subject of interest
- creative with problem solving
- good in a crisis
- hyperfocus
- working under pressure.

Many people with ADHD have issues with clutter and hoarding; they do not necessarily have an emotional attachment to their belongings but find the thought process of deciding what to keep, donate and/or recycle completely overwhelming. People with ADHD quite often don't see the mess, but recognize their difficulty in finding things because of it – hence the term 'clutter blindness'.

Issues with 'messiness' are typical for ADHDers. The idea of putting things away in a cupboard feels like putting things in a black hole. Piles of things are dotted around ADHDers' homes, although the idea of putting things in a pile can also be anxiety-provoking as they do not know what is hidden at the bottom of the pile.

The power of the pile

Looking through neurotypical eyes, the term 'piler, not filer' is sometimes applied to someone whose home is full of piles of objects, almost like 'molehills'. For the 'piler', each pile represents an action, a specific category, a specific piece of research or important piece of information. Mixing the piles around is like emptying out a filing cabinet and messing everything around.

ADHDers are lateral spreaders – they spread their belongings out so they can see them. It is actually very difficult to protect space. Any space we have, we fill. For example, I use an ironing board at Christmas to wrap presents. If I were to leave the ironing board out, I am sure it would be used as a surface on which to 'plonk' things down.

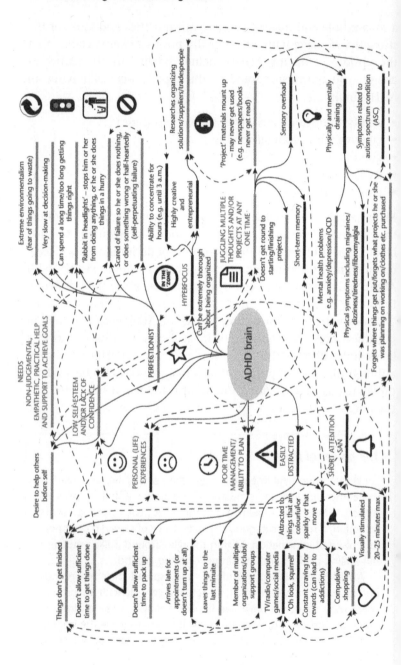

There are many celebrities with ADHD in the world of drama and performing arts, and some acknowledge their ADHD in terms of the creativity that the condition brings but also the burnout that can result. ADHDers develop strategies to manage their symptoms. Many need to compensate by working extra hard to achieve the grades they need, use timers and alarms to make sure they arrive on time, and have cues to remember to do certain tasks.

Did you know?

There are many famous athletes and sportspersons with ADHD who see their ADHD as a superpower. They thrive under pressure and use their hyperfocus to concentrate on the game ahead. Michael Phelps is one of them – an American swimmer who has won 19 Olympic medals. He channelled his energy in the swimming pool. He could not concentrate in the classroom but could in the swimming pool.

Autistic spectrum disorder (ASD)

The National Autistic Society (NAS) defines autism as 'a lifelong developmental disability which affects how people communicate and interact with the world'. The NAS states: 'More than one in 100 people are on the autism spectrum, and there are round 700,000 autistic adults and children in the UK.'

Presentations of autism vary widely, but may be characterized by:

- difficulties with interacting in a social setting and interpreting non-verbal or verbal communication and unwritten rules in a neurotypical world
- intense and passionate and perhaps obscure interests and hobbies
- being challenged by sensory issues, such as sounds, smells and crowded places, as well as information-processing issues
- repetitive behaviours and rituals
- struggles with changes in routine and environment and any last-minute change of plan or route or cancellation
- difficulties with decision making, planning, prioritizing and organization.

Because it is a *spectrum* disorder the characteristics may vary from being mild to severe. ASD is now the umbrella term that covers all level of autism. Asperger's syndrome is no longer recognized as a diagnosis and now comes under the ASD umbrella term, although individuals may still refer to themselves as 'aspies'.

The UK naturalist, campaigner and broadcaster Chris Packham has done much to raise awareness of the complexities of autism, and has been involved with the NAS as well as a couple of documentaries on autism. He describes that his experience of walking in woodland as very different from that of someone who is neurotypical. What he sees is different: he doesn't just see trees, he sees the different types of tree, and wonders what their scientific Latin names are; he wonders how they connect with each other and where their roots might lead; he asks himself what insects and animals might be inhabiting the trees. It is no surprise that the world for neurodivergent people can be overwhelming. For someone who is neurotypical a walk in the woods might mean an experience of peace, calm and lushness.

Through COVID-19, I kept up our telephone support groups for those with hoarding behaviours and found that the issues we were supporting clients with were not necessarily those of hoarding and having too much stuff, but more around the sudden changes the government was making in the rules of social distancing, when you were allowed out, what a 'bubble' consisted of, and so on.

When I am working with colleagues and working with clients, I can often observe their minds whirling with questions and almost feel as if I can hear their thoughts being formulated. 'Information overload' is a real thing, especially for the neurodiverse community – we will look at fact hoarding in Chapter 4.

Disorganization can play a huge part in the life of someone identified as having ASD, as research has suggested that up to 80 per cent of these individuals will experience difficulties with executive functioning (EF). This refers to the functions of the brain that involve attention, memory, organization, time management, planning, initiation and goal setting among others. We will be look at this topic in more detail in Chapter 3.

Did you know?

Masking/camouflaging is a technique used by some autistic/menopausal/ADHD people to help them fit in and function in social and work settings.

One of the difficulties ASD can present is giving eye contact. Chris Packham is quoted as saying: 'Talking to a TV camera is much easier as it's just a piece of glass. It's the evolution of masking.'

Many clients will exhibit not only hoarding behaviours but both ADS and ADHD. There are many similarities between ASD and ADHD, and the conditions may be genetic. Obsessive compulsive disorder (OCD) can also play into the mix but some of the behaviour traits of ASD and ADHD may include obsessive behaviours around routine, collections and rituals.

Helen's story

Helen's story shows us how complex the causes of CD behaviours can be. There is rarely one simple cause, but a network of factors and triggers. In Helen's case a diagnosis of ADHD was the beginning of a gradual realization of what drives her behaviours and how she might deal with them.

I am nearly 54 years old now and I live and work in Liverpool, UK. I have a daughter who is now 33 years old and lives independently in an adapted bungalow 20 minutes away. We are very close and spend time together regularly.

I grew up in a small family terrace with my mum, my dad and a little sister. We did not have much money but had lots of love and stability.

Having anything new was a big event, rare and special – a new outfit for a wedding, a new sofa, Christmas and birthdays. Most of what we had was second-hand or a make-do until we could afford anything better. Dad was my hero – a man-mountain but flawed. He had a secretive gambling addition that affected him and us for the rest of his life.

Growing up, me and my sister had jobs to do – I hated washing up, dusting. It always made me sneeze. I liked making all the beds and ironing, though. I went through lots of tea sets with my clumsiness, and I also remember making lots of mess and having big tidy-ups.

I got married young, 20 years old, nearly 21. Our first home needed lots of work. I enjoyed collecting stuff for my 'bottom drawer'. Making all the soft furnishings and cushions, curtains. The Birmingham rag market was a regular haunt. My husband was very organized and the complete opposite to me.

I remember, one day, I had dusted the fireplace and put two of his military figurines back in the wrong position. I then watched in disbelief as he got our measuring tape to check the alignment to the carriage clock!

For me there was a trigger that started my hoarding. It was the traumatic birth of our daughter and the subsequent physical and mental damage from that. She was left with cerebral palsy, and I got sepsis and post-partum psychosis. I was treated in various hospitals for the first three months of her life. Separated from her, things were very tough for my new little family coping with the trauma, a disabled child and I also felt the pressure to cope or be seen to be able to cope in case they put me back in hospital again. I developed a mistrust and fear of doctors after that. Not surprisingly, our marriage failed. It was a painful time, and my focus was my daughter. I took comfort in buying her toys and clothes. When we got divorced, I moved with her to a two-bedroom ground-floor flat nearby. I still live there today.

Emotionally I would feel secure and safe there, and however fleetingly [I had] a feeling of excitement acquiring something new and also becoming overwhelmed by it and would often get frustrated when I couldn't find anything. My routine would be chaotic – laundry and washing up would pile up for days on end. At times I would try and have big clear-ups throughout my daughter's life. She would often recall these and feel sad when they didn't last and that things would often get messy again. Now I was a single parent, money was tight making me terrified of parting with anything in case I couldn't afford to replace it. So acquiring, not letting go, and having no set routine became the norm.

I would often collect lots of books and magazines, some of which were about lovely homes or organizing and decluttering. I had lots of clothes but felt I had nothing to wear, a lot of food but no meals to make, lots of crafting materials but nothing to create. I was never content and felt I needed more. Homeware was a big thing I kept acquiring and ended up with enough linen to restock a small hotel. Cushions were also a big thing that I constantly kept acquiring; I became the family joke when I finally cleared them and let go of three large sacks full of cushions and pads.

Hoarding like this carried on for a large number of years, getting much worse when my daughter left home at 18 to go to residential college. I had tried to keep a lid on it while she lived with me, fearing losing her or social services taking her away from me if I didn't. We led a double life – outwardly keeping up appearances but at home struggling in the cluttered chaotic environment, fearful and ashamed, unable to ask for any help.

It was around that time I had a period of depression. I can only describe it as like trying to walk through thick black mud and fog – everything took way too much energy and I just wanted to sleep all the time.

With my daughter gone, perimenopause started. It was a stressful time: My dad was diagnosed with cancer, and I faced ongoing stress, bullying and changes at work. This was now the norm. I had got to the point where very often my living spaces were taken over with lots of clutter, random stuff, everything everywhere, and this often would stop me using the space as I should have: sleeping in my bedroom, cooking meals in my kitchen, relaxing or socializing in my lounge. I had now crossed the line. I was a hoarder, very ashamed of what I had become and the way I was existing – certainly not living. I tried everything to hide it, avoided anyone coming round to my home, and just tried to stay out as much as possible.

I hated living and feeling like this. I hated myself even more. I always say now whatever you think of people who hoard … they will think of themselves 100 times more. It certainly felt true to me. I felt overwhelmed by the sheer volume of the task of reclaiming any space. I often intended to clear my clutter. Every New Year it would be my resolution, but I would often fail, quickly give up, exhausted and frustrated with myself. Why can't I do this? What's so wrong with me? Why am I the only one in the world who can't do it? Or so I thought.

My daughter went on to university and finally had her own bungalow to live in. I felt my hoarding contributed to driving her away. [I felt] a failure, hating the way I lived, if you could call it that. I was at rock bottom. Sometimes my family tried to help – this just made me feel even worse when things would soon pile up again and I then felt as if I had let them down as well as myself. I know they meant well but ultimately the change had to come from myself.

I just didn't know how I would overcome this. I felt I was drowning in stuff, spending money replacing lost things I couldn't find – often slipping and falling over things lying around.

It was at this point in our lives the amazing Folly came into my daughter's life. Dogs are wonderful positive beings. From the get-go she brought joy, love and freedom with her. She is my daughter's everything. I saw that joy and love and as a walker and volunteer for the Greyhound Trust myself, I dared to dream of that kind of love for myself.

Eventually I adopted a beautiful dog called Shelley and within six months of having him I was off all antidepressants. It was also at this time I watched a programme with my daughter on hoarding and it was about a mother and daughter – [the TV and radio presenter] Jasmine Harman – and their story. It struck a chord as the programme addressed the impact a mother's hoarding had had on her daughter growing up and the struggles they were having trying to address it. It touched me deeply and it opened a tricky conversation with my own daughter. She wanted to help despite her own limits and promised to support me in this struggle and help end it. She found a support group that had only just started the month before run by two members of the team from a local fire station.

I went along to it, promising my daughter I would try it. Walking through the door took courage. I had convinced myself I would be in a room with a load of firefighters all telling me off for being a fire hazard. I couldn't have been more wrong. I was welcomed into a room (no firefighters!) and met other hoarders and their loved ones for the first time. Tea and biscuits were put in front of us as we shared our stories. For the first time I saw I was not alone in this. I got very emotional. From then on I didn't want to miss it and would try and attend every monthly meeting. My daughter came to some of them with me and shared with me the impact the hoarding had on her – it was difficult to hear. She gave me lots of encouragement and celebrated every success.

In the group we looked at lots of practical ways to change, tips and tricks were shared, experiences and successes celebrated. I soon started to realize lasting change. I would tell people about the group and openly talk about what I was doing with friends, family, even colleagues, I adopted ideas that worked for me. For example, I would throw rubbish out and put out the donations in the charity bags before I went to work and dropped them off on my way home at the local centres after work. I would reward myself by watching a film or TV programme and would quickly notice a difference when I returned home. My dream was to have a bedroom like a hotel room. I enjoyed sharing this success with the group too. I am on a journey – it was hard at times, at other times easy – and I wasn't on my own. It became part of my routine. I made my bed every day. I constantly revisited areas, reducing, reorganizing as I went. It has been like peeling layers from an onion.

I couldn't find things to start with and would wander all around the flat looking for something and then laugh at myself when I found it in its 'home' – the last place I would think to find it. Now I go there automatically and smile at myself.

It's a joy now. Before now, I would often wander into a room, look at it and go back out again. Now I open wardrobes, cupboards, drawers – I take down tins from the kitchen cupboards I hadn't used before.[Previously] my home would be like an explosion in Primark with a floordrobe and a bedrobe situation.

Lots has changed – not just my home. I went back to a church I used to visit. I have been diagnosed with ADHD. I have always known about ADHD and always thought I might be a square peg going into a round hole and now realize the diagnosis has helped me recognize why I found things difficult. My mum and dad told me what to do, my husband too, but once divorced I had no one telling me what to do; I was like a child in a sweet shop. I indulged in every interest, every curiosity and every passion, and many of my collections stemmed and developed from then on.

With the ADHD diagnosis, I found it very hard to accept the time I had lost struggling with day-to-day life. Many of us ADHDers talk a lot about the time we lose trying to find things and time lost with loved ones. I had been struggling in the dark for so long, and now the light was on and I had found the light switch. I also see my superpowers such as the hyperfocus. I noticed that I do not respond to being told what to do and I understand that is part of the ADHD – not wanting to follow instructions. Criticism is hard as is my own self-criticism, so I have been practising self-compassion for a while. Rewards are something relatively new, and focusing on the achievements no matter how small is a big game changer. Even the language I use with myself has changed – rather than say 'I am going to tackle my bedroom', I now say 'I am just going to sort this little bit out'. I am now stopping and noticing how I am. Dopamine fixes are that much more lasting after I have decluttered – it isn't just a short fix; it feels like a continual high.

I couldn't show emotions and suppressed any meltdowns, and on losing the plot, I would show no tears or upset. I wore a veil over who I truly was. My coach asked me to try and not mask. I am not sure I know how to because I have been doing it for so long. However, I am now really quite bubbly and the first to cry and show rage. I took to self-acceptance and being comfortable with my ADHDness.

I have a deep mistrust of medications stemming back to the birth of my daughter and the errors the medical professionals made at that time, so for me I did not want to have any medication for ADHD. If I can try and do without medication, I would prefer to do that first. Regardless of if you are on medication or not, we still need to build strategies and know our triggers. Know your 'wall of awful'. Paperwork is an issue, and I am thinking of asking for support with this.

I used to play games with myself – how many things can I pick up during the ad break? Can I empty the dishwasher while the kettle is boiling? Making it playful and indulging in fidget toys and being open about it and not hiding them away. Why should we stop playing now we are grown-ups? My confidence has grown, and I take pride in my home. I dress for the part. I have an apron – linen – and when I wear it, I am Mrs Tidy Big, and I feel as if I am in business.

Becoming more aware of those times I was craving crappy food, needing a sweet snack, dashing out to some random shops. I noticed this and wanted to look at what gave me a high. It has been a bit of a self-discovery, and I think having more self-awareness has helped me with self-regulation.

I survived a pandemic. Sadly I lost my beautiful dog to liver disease but celebrate the love and joy he unconditionally gave to me for seven wonderful years. I've been on the TV, on BBC Breakfast news twice talking about hoarding, had interviews on radio, newspapers and a photoshoot too. Knowledge is power.

I just wanted to give back and decided to begin one-to-one support helping others. I have been privileged to have worked with lots of people at the start of their own journeys, and I also started a group of us coming together in the hope of helping each other. Opening Doors is at the early stages but I hope it will grow. It is made up of three or four liked-minded people taking it in turns to visit each other's homes. I still develop new interests – currently it's watercolour paintings and tai chi and singing my heart out in the amazing community choir where we have chances to perform. Last year I was at the Commonwealth Games opening ceremony. I am comfortable with the gifts and curses of my ADHD and thankful too for the insight and powers of observation that are my superpowers. My home nurtures me; I feel grateful and thankful I live in it. Who knows what life has in store? But watch this space – anything wonderful could happen.

Perfectionism

Perfectionists not only create unrealistic, impossible and unrelenting high standards for themselves but also for others and this can be particularly difficult when you are working with someone with these tendencies as they can be quick to find fault, criticize and create snag lists that will drive people away from wanting to help them. Their own tendencies to inwardly berate themselves and be self-critical are often linked to self-limiting core beliefs such as 'I am useless' or 'I can never get anything right ...'

Many people affected by CD and too much stuff are perfectionists, and this is a trait to be aware of in yourself or if you are helping someone else. Perfectionism can:

- lead to procrastination and paralysis – if you wait to do something perfectly, you may never get anything done and for some of us nothing gets started for a fear of failure
- make us indecisive – if we fear making the wrong decision, we make no decision because of the uncertainty of having the right outcome
- deter progress by causing us to focus too readily on insignificant details and therefore fail to see the bigger picture
- deter any progress in addressing CD behaviours, especially on the days when energy and moods might be low.

One example of perfectionism in a hoarding situation would be where a person does not want to put their clothes and bedclothes away because they still need ironing. The reality is that it would take several hours to iron them, so rather than putting them away and ironing them as and when they are needed (as a nonperfectionist might), the perfectionist leaves them out and simply blocks them out. The same can be said for someone who has not done any filing for years because they have not found a perfect filing system.

Issues around perfectionism are on the increase, especially with socially mediated pressures to have the perfect home, perfect body, perfect life. Thomas Curran, author of *The Perfection Trap*, has spent over ten years researching the subject and explains that our 'dangerous' quest for perfectionism can impact on our mental wellbeing and massively increase our anxiety. Curran has given an illuminating TED Talk on perfectionism and its harms that is worth checking out.[4] He stresses that striving for excellence is a very different thing from striving for the perfect – one that allows us to fail, be kind to ourselves and be good enough.

As I have found with many of my clients, perfectionism is often linked with OCD and OCPD as well with adverse childhood

---

[4] https://www.ted.com/talks/thomas_curran_our_dangerous_obsession_with_perfectionism_is_getting_worse

experiences and not feeling good enough. It can be an addiction, too, like any other – we often talk about 'recovering perfectionists', 'letting it go' and being a 'good-enougher'. As an article on Curran's ideas in UK newspaper *The Guardian* put it: 'When the dust settles, perfectionists often have little more to show for their pain than those who go "easy".'[5]

Here are some tips on how we can overcome perfectionism:

- Cultivate resilience – don't allow yourself to be crushed by failure
- Practise mindfulness, self-compassion and self-awareness
- Strive but do not over-strive
- Know that you are enough and have enough
- Learn to delegate
- Ask for help
- Think in other colours, not just in black and white – there is no right or wrong way of doing something
- Recognize that there may be an ideal world but that you should also see the reality of a situation
- Be prepared to make – and learn from – your mistakes
- Accept that you cannot always be in control of any given situation
- Learn to tolerate discomfort
- There doesn't have to be the perfect win – there is bronze and silver as well as gold.

Chronic overwhelm

Many of us can feel overwhelmed at any given time, and it can take just one small thing to tip us over the edge. Overwhelm can affect anyone – regardless of the diagnosis, whether it's depression, an excessive workload, ADHD, empty nest syndrome, major life events, a job loss. It could be triggered by a lost earring, accidentally deleting two thousand words of the book you are writing, missing the last post.

---

[5] Will Coldwell, 'The rise of perfectionism – and the harm it's doing us all', *The Guardian*, 4 June 2023.

Some mental health issues also trigger overwhelm – long-term stress, depression, obsessive compulsive disorder, any anxiety-based disorders and trauma. We can all experience overwhelm, and with that comes the sense that we find it difficult to cope with day-to-day mundane tasks and so put off difficult jobs. The feeling of overwhelm can certainly be experienced by those with hoarding behaviours, having too much stuff and clutter.

Overwhelm can feel like we are being saturated by negative thoughts, feelings and emotions. Some of the symptoms can be physical such as rapid heartbeat, breathing difficulties, panic attacks and stomach-related issues.

We may freeze – a normal response to stress and overwhelm. We may feel pessimistic, feel unable to rationalize and feel that small tasks are insurmountable. You may feel irritable, unable to sleep and put off and postpone appointments with friends or dental/eye appointments. Reactions to situations such as losing keys or burning your breakfast toast may well become disproportionate.

Did you know?

Churning is the act of moving things around without getting rid of anything. This is a regular activity of someone with hoarding behaviours. We can emotionally churn as well as physically churn by the act of turning things over and over in our minds as well as in our homes.

The spoon theory

The spoon theory has only superficially anything to do with spoons. The theory was created by Christine Miserandino, an award-winning US chronic illness blogger and patient advocate, in 2003. Christine has lupus, an autoimmune disease. While out at dinner, her friend asked her what it was like to live with the condition. Christine did not feel able to articulate just how difficult it was but wanted to illustrate how her condition impacted on her life. She grabbed every spoon she could find and explained to her friend how each spoon represented one unit of energy.

Each spoon represents currency. Each spoon – and it doesn't matter if we are using a teaspoon, a serving spoon or a soup spoon – is used as a token of energy, whether it is physical, mental or emotional. Energy to get out of bed, have a shower, ring the plumber, make breakfast, or open the post. The theory was originally taken up by groups with autoimmune and chronic illnesses, but has since become more widely used in online mental health and neurodivergent communities.

The spoon theory is a great way to help people who are impacted by a limited amount of energy, whether it is a physical health condition, a neurological condition, depression, or any state of mental wellbeing. We can use the spoon theory to manage our own anxiety, pain and energy. Our sense of wellness can be impacted by anything from a bad night's sleep, overwhelm from a trip to the supermarket or a thoughtless negative comment to feeling fed up because it's raining.

How many spoons we each have can vary from person to person, day to day. Some of us will not even think about how many spoons we have or need, and have a whole drawerful at our disposal! For some people mental and/or physical energy, stamina and motivation may well be low and they may feel as though they have no spoons at all.

Filling in a new passport application or wrapping a parcel to take to the post office for some may take one spoon; for others it may take more. Different tasks and activities will take different amounts of spoons depending on how we are challenged by day-to-day tasks. For some the idea of going out at the end of the day for drinks with friends will feel too much, too draining or too tiring – more spoons than we have. We can decide how many spoons we have at the start of the day and how we are going to use them.

We may well run out of spoons and so try to use spoons from the next day's quota. This, however, is like leaning into your overdraft, so I think it's important to look at how we replenish our stash of spoons – perhaps by taking a nap or a walk, or doing any type of mindful activity. It's helpful to manage the number of spoons you have as this helps us be realistic about how much we can achieve or do. There is a hashtag used on social media – #Spoonies – which helps bring together people who are challenged by managing their emotional, mental and physical energy. The Spoon Theory has really helped raise awareness that we cannot take for granted that we all have ample energy to manage day-to-day life.

I am an introvert and recognize that if I have been around people all day, whether it is a social occasion or work related, I need to manage my spoons. Quite often, bright lights, noisy coffee machines and crowded shops can leave me feeling depleted. I also recognize that I am a morning person, so I need fewer spoons in the morning to achieve difficult jobs than I do in the afternoon.

If we are running low on spoons and feel we want to cancel meeting a friend, rather than use an excuse, using the spoon theory is more honest. So, you might say, 'I'm running low on spoons, do you mind if we reschedule?' This helps our friends understand how we are feeling, rather than thinking we are flaky and unreliable. It is also helpful for colleagues to appreciate that we all require a different amount of spoons to perform a task, undertake an engagement and manage the challenges of day-to-day life.

Rumination and looping thoughts

We can all experience ruminating thoughts where thoughts are go round and round in a spiral. Such thoughts can be triggered by fears, phobias and addictions, as well as by specific stressful events such as a sudden and unexpected relationship breakdown, a traumatic event such as an accident, waiting for a mortgage approval, the results of an exam or a medical screening, or perfectionism. Rumination is typically found in people with obsessive compulsive disorder (OCD) and obsessive compulsive personality disorder (OCPD).

I have worked with many clients who are focused on what might go wrong, and this can be debilitating and very much connected with their anxiety and chronic sense of overwhelm.

By default our brains are wired to negative thinking, and we all have an internal critic we carry around with us.

Linked to rumination is 'looping', or recurring, thoughts, which can be linked to OCD and depression. A bereavement may bring looping thoughts of 'I should have done and said ...'. A relationship breakdown may bring looping thoughts of 'if I had been more ..., he/she would not have left'. We can become stuck in a thought loop.

Five takeaways

1 There are many contributing factors and triggers connected with chronic disorganization – being aware of which of them contribute to your own or other's CD can help you begin to address its effects.

2 Often people have a complex network of contributing factors, although it may take a trigger such as a bereavement to cause disorganization to become chronic – that is entrenched and disabling.

3 Attention deficit hyperactivity disorder (ADHD) is often found in people with CD – if you think this may apply to you or a person you are helping, it is well worth getting a diagnosis.

4 Whether you are on medication or not, you need to build strategies and know your triggers. Know your 'wall of awful'.

5 You can change the wiring of your brain and change your habits and behaviours – practices such as mindfulness and meditation can help you along the way.

3

Neurodiversity and executive functions

Understanding that we are all unique, that our brains are wired differently, and that we think and process events and information differently is the first step in accepting the world of neurodiversity. Essentially, the term 'neurodiversity' reflects the 'diversity' of our minds. We see things through different lenses. We experience, respond and interact with the world differently. There is no right or left way of thinking, learning and behaving.

The concept of neurodiversity was conceived by the Australian sociologist Judy Singer in 1998. She noticed that her daughter had very similar traits to her own mother who had survived the Holocaust. Her daughter was diagnosed with what was then called Asperger's, and Singer likewise describes herself as likely to be somewhere on the autistic spectrum. Historically, neurodiversity used to be considered negatively and as a hindrance/disorder, but it now considered more neutrally, with both challenges and strengths.

Some of the neurological conditions that are often referred to as 'neurodiverse' are:

- autistic spectrum disorder (ASD)
- ADD/ADHD – attention deficit disorder/attention deficit hyperactivity disorder
- dyslexia, dyscalculia, dyspraxia (DCD), dysgraphia
- misophonia
- Tourette's syndrome (and other tic disorders).

There are lots of conditions that overlap. The biggest thing we can do is to be more sensitive, thoughtful and accommodating of neurodiversity. Awareness and empathy are key to improving neurodivergent people's day-to-day functioning. We can also be considerate of people's learning styles (see Chapter 7) and forms of communication when we are supporting neurodivergents.

The cognitive functions of neurodivergent people are different, and they may display certain behavioural traits including difficulty with organizing, planning and time management; however, they may thrive on retaining vast amounts of information and are good at attention to detail, often volunteering to research the best vacuum cleaner, deodorant, venue and so on (see Chapter 1). They are often very strong in certain functions and very challenged in others, compared to a neurotypical person who will usually be fairly average across all functions.

Many neurodiverse conditions are hereditary, and often adults will recognize their own condition only when their children are diagnosed.

Research indicates that acquired conditions and cognitive changes can impact on our behaviours and cognition, and these conditions include long COVID, long-term stress, PTSD and menopause among others. These conditions and changes can increase the challenges of executive functions (see below), exacerbate symptoms, and make them more noticeable.

Adaptations

Many strides are being taken in raising awareness of, educating people about and making adaptations for neurodiversity in what is essentially a neurotypical world. One family I am working with includes two young boys both with an ADHD diagnosis, and they have a therapy dog at home. Trains are now equipped with 'quiet carriages', supermarkets accommodate 'quiet shopping times' and cinemas have 'relaxed' screenings. In the workplace, policies are now in place to accommodate the needs of neurodivergent employees and reasonable adjustments are being put in place. In the training arena, materials are printed using dyslexia-friendly coloured papers and fonts. People can wear lanyards in the workplace and in public, indicating that they have a 'hidden disability' and may need support, understanding and more time. Some employees are exempt from 'hot desking' and given their own car parking space.

Neurodiverse conditions manifest themselves in different ways and can impact on our executive functions, which can make day-to-day tasks very challenging. Challenges include:

- forgetting to do tasks such as turning off the oven
- difficulty measuring and managing time
- following through on instructions and directions
- taking longer to process information.

We all, however, have our strengths and weaknesses in these areas of functioning, and these play a big part in managing our daily lives. This is particularly relevant to people with hoarding behaviours and chronic disorganization, who have difficulty with organization, categorization and regulating thoughts, directions and behaviours, as well as with memory and focus.

Where possible, I prefer to use more positive language around neurodiversity, and will try to refer to 'challenges' rather than 'weaknesses'. I think it's important to focus on our strengths and recognize the support and strategies we may need in place if we are to overcome the challenges we may struggle with every day.

What are executive functions?

Executive functions are the set of skills we use to plan, manage and organize our daily lives. Put simply, they refer to how we get things done and what is needed to get things done. These skills are controlled by an area in our brain called the frontal lobe which is considered to be the part of the brain that, if you were to use a metaphor, is the chief executive which governs all the other departments. The brain's frontal lobe controls our executive functions and does not fully develop until we reach our mid-twenties.

There are various thoughts as to how many executive functions there are and what they are called but I have based mine on the model developed by Drs Peg Dawson and Richard Guare.[1] There are different terms used to describe them but I have chosen the following:

---

[1] See, for example, their website smartbutscatteredkids.com and their book *The Smart But Scattered Guide to Success: How to Use Your Brain's Executive Skills to Keep Up, Stay Calm, and Get Organized at Work and at Home* (Guilford Press, 2015).

1 self-control	7 organization
2 working memory	8 stress tolerance
3 emotional regulation	9 time management
4 task initiation	10 cognitive flexibility
5 sustained attention	11 goal perseverance
6 prioritization and planning	12 self-awareness

We'll look at each of these in turn, though you will notice that many of them feed into each other. Becoming aware of your own relationship with and performance in each of these functions and across the board can be key to improving them and thereby helping you address CD behaviours (among others). Throughout, you'll find strategies to help you do this.

EXECUTIVE FUNCTIONS

Self-control
Working memory
Emotional regulation
Task initiation
Sustained attention
Planning/prioritizing
Organization
Time management
Cognitive flexibility
Self-awareness
Goal perseverance
Stress tolerance

1 Self-control

This is the ability to pause and think before responding and acting so as to create responses that are reasonable. Some might relate this to 'impulse control'. If you lack this function, or it is undeveloped, you may make snap judgements, and you may find it difficult not to interrupt or think things through before blurting things out. You may snap.

Strategies for improving your self-control to situations start with having some self-awareness of your reactions, acknowledging your behaviour and readdressing your response to it. You can turn things around, and with habit it becomes easier. My mantra is: Don't react, respond. Breathe deeply before responding to a stressful situation. Follow a mantra such as the Serenity Prayer, learning to acknowledge and accept what you can and cannot control.

Recognize how your behaviours make you feel. Meditation and a good walk can often help rebalance our response to situations.

Again, mindfulness is helpful in these situations, as are yoga and daily affirmations. There are many apps that can help calm your mind.

2 Working memory

Working memory is the ability to recall, remember, retain and work with information required to work across various tasks, especially on a short-term basis – knowing, for example, where you put your phone or keys down. I think this function is the most significantly impaired in all the clients whom I have worked with over the years.

If this is an area of difficulty for you, you may forget what you were doing because of a distraction or be absent-minded. For example, you may forget where you have parked your car or leave your car keys at the supermarket check-out. You might go upstairs to your bedroom to fetch a cardigan, notice that the plants need watering, water them and then come back downstairs having forgotten why you went up upstairs in the first place. The expression 'It goes in one ear and out the other' relates not so much to people not listening but not being able to *retain* the information. Directions and instructions can be difficult as can keeping track of what's what.

Having visual clues can really help with remembering about the task in hand, what needs to happen that day. The use of sticky notes (as large and as brightly coloured as possible) can act as a really useful aide-memoire. Laminated lists or printed lists, too, can help with tasks such as food shopping and packing to go away on holiday.

Creating a structure and routine to your day can help, as can breaking tasks down into manageable chunks – called 'chunking'. Chunking helps you to avoid multitasking. Stay on one task, on one area, one item, at any one time.

The use of a mobile phone to set alarms for scheduled tasks can be helpful, too. Taking photographs of items on your phone can also act as a useful prompt (e.g. a picture of the location of your car in the airport car park). Create a checklist, too, to remind yourself to feed the dog, reply to emails, put the rubbish out.

The use of a song, a rhyme or an acronym can help with remembering information. To remember my car registration, I have created a rhyme, and I have learned my mobile number by singing it.

3 Emotional regulation

This is also known as emotional control or self-regulation. Emotional regulation is the ability to manage and keep your emotions under control and stay calm, especially in the event of unscheduled or unexpected setbacks that may prevent a task being completed. People who are challenged with emotional control overly worry, and are challenged by handling quick changes in their emotions. Many neurodivergent people are unable to identify what emotion they are feeling and find it hard to explain their emotions to others.

Did you know?

Alexithymia is a term used when someone is unable able to identify, express and/or name their emotions. It is a common among people with ASD but is also quite widely found in men who conform to 'traditional' norms of masculinity where showing emotion is often seen as weakness.

If this is an area that you do not function well in, you may find it difficult to manage your feelings and thoughts, and make poor decisions when under stress. Impulsive behaviour is a trait often found in someone challenged around emotional regulation. If you are not challenged in this area, you may be able to respond calmly and make good decisions in times of stress and be moderate and measured.

The ability to pause before reacting to a situation is a skill to be practised as way of helping to control our behaviours, impulses and emotions. It helps us develop resilience, stay true to our values and be mindful of our responses to difficult situations, uncomfortable feelings and everchanging circumstances.

The COVID-19 pandemic made many of us mindful of having to endure difficult circumstances, and here mindfulness is a useful strategy. According to Dr Jon Kabat-Zinn, founder of Mindfulness-Based Stress Reduction (MBSR), mindfulness is 'the awareness that arises from paying attention, on purpose, in the present moment and non-judgementally'.[2]

Reframing is another useful tactic. We all know the expressions seeing your 'glass half full' or 'glass half empty' referring to having a positive or negative outlook – but what matters really is the ability to say to oneself: 'At least I have a glass, irrespective of whether it is half empty or half full.' Learning to breathe, pause and find gratitude helps put space between our thoughts and reactions to our thoughts. 'Thoughts are just thoughts.' Learning to reset is a strategy worth developing. As the American psychiatrist Viktor Frankl famously wrote: 'Forces beyond your control can take away everything you possess except one thing, your freedom to choose how you will respond to the situation. You cannot control what happens to you in life, but you can always control what you will feel and do about what happens to you.'[3]

Learning to control our emotions is a real strength, and the ability to acknowledge difficult thoughts and feelings rather than avoid them is a skill that, with routine and structure present, can be further developed.

---

[2] J. Kabat-Zinn (2003), 'Mindfulness-Based Interventions in Context Past, Present, and Future', *Clinical Psychology Science and Practice*, 10, 144–56, at p. 145.

[3] Viktor E. Frankl, *Man's Search for Meaning* (original Ger., 1946; original Eng. trans., 1959; Boston Press, 2014), p. x.

4 Task initiation

This can also be referred to, or better identified as, self-motivation or self-activation. It's the ability to get started on a job you know you need to do but don't really want to do and have difficulty making that first step. For many, this means that they experience procrastination and avoidance tactics. Deadlines can often work to get someone started.

If this is a function that is impaired, you may procrastinate, put things off until the last minute and then ask for an extension. You may not be able to start immediately on a project and then find it difficult to start and need a deadline. You may be put off by challenging tasks, not want to get started for fear of not doing it perfectly. The fear of not completing a task perfectly can act as a barrier to getting started at all (see the discussion of perfectionism in Chapter 2). Overthinking and being obsessive and the challenges that this brings can also be a hindrance to getting started. OCD can impact on someone's ability to get started through the thoughts and fears that prevail – 'What if this happens?' Thinking through the worst-case scenario can cause someone to go into freeze mode.

Many of us can relate to this – putting off a task because it might be dull or overwhelming, or just feels too big. As we have seen, 'chunking' can help here: looking at the step in front rather than the whole staircase. We need to understand what our sub-conscious might be saying too – we create unconscious scenarios and stories in our heads – scenarios and stories that are just stories about possible outcomes, barriers, failures, fears.

Learning to work when your energy is best and setting the scene can be useful. Limit the time you spend on it. Recognize your feelings towards why you might be putting something off. Is it because you do not feel qualified or confident enough? The task feels too overwhelming and quite often we avoid a task because of the uncomfortable feelings attached to it. Procrastination and perfectionism go hand in hand. Remember: 'Done is better than perfect.'

5 Sustained attention

This refers to the ability to stay focused on a task until it is complete, knowing that it requires effort and attention. It also involves the need to control impulses and avoid distractions so the task can be completed without flitting from one activity to another. In the face of modern technological distractions – such as social media – it is no wonder that we struggle with filling in forms, finishing books and feeding the cat. What with smartphone notifications, X (formerly Twitter) and Facebook feeds, emails, texts and WhatsApp messages, 24-hour news updates, and so on, we are frazzled. There is so much noise – which is not even noise in the real sense of the word – that it can be hard to stay on task without going down a path that leads to many other paths, leaving us wondering what on earth the path was we were on in the first place!

If this is a function that is impacted, you may find it hard to filter out distractions to get the task done and dusted. Completing a tax return or filling in a passport form requires attention, focus and concentration as well as time.

If this is an area of difficulty for you, you may get easily distracted and move on to something else, find it hard to get back into a task once distracted, flit between tasks, or find it difficult to stay on a task.

As I've said earlier, I call sometimes my clients 'butterflies' as they flutter between jobs. But there's also another reason: ultimately, there can be transformation, too, when we adapt strategies to overcome these hurdles. Some of these are:

Pairing up with a 'buddy' can really help with maintaining focus on a task. The 'buddy' should ideally be there as a silent partner, acting as a body double. Their presence alone helps sustain commitment to the task in hand. It helps keep up motivation and keep the person on track and focused.

Building in a reward system – for example having a warm, comforting drink and then coming back to the task.

Removing distractions by clearing your desk and turning your phone off, along with any email or social media notifications. Using a timer to see how much you can get done in a set time can also be a helpful strategy. If the tasks are tedious, music can act as a boost to energy or commitment or help sustain your attention.

My friend Amanda often comes to my home to co-work with me and we use each other's energy and accountability to complete any life admin and work admin that we are taxed by. Sometimes Amanda might say, 'Shall we have a drink now?' and I will answer, 'Let's wait until our break at 11 am.' Lunch is always a treat because we have worked really hard and that is our reward.

Acknowledging the drivers for our behaviours is really useful, as is knowing that we use distractions to detract from discomfort.

6 Planning/prioritizing

This is the ability to make decisions, to know the steps needed, and recognize the tools required without jumping straight in. A plan involves identifying the end goal, and understanding the sequence of the plan and what is included in that plan. This skill is one that needs practice, so it's no wonder there are jobs specially created for this area, such as project managers, relocation experts, virtual personal assistants (VPAs) and organizers. There is an abundance of books on the subject, too. For some, getting started can be easy but finishing a project can be a struggle and prioritizing the steps needed can be difficult.

I like to use the analogy of moving house and the steps and priorities needed to achieve this goal, and, house moving, like any project, is very much about figuring out the start, the end and all the steps in-between.

I consider planning and prioritizing one of my strengths and actually embrace the challenge of a project – whether it is selling a house, renovating a bathroom, or getting ticket machines installed on the railway line between London and Brighton. I used to work in project management with Network Rail and believe I acquired and developed a huge number of skills that I now apply not only in my work life but also in my home life. Planning and prioritizing rely on many of the other executive functions to see a goal through.

I see this as an area many clients ask for my help with, as they struggle to get to the finish line without getting bogged down and overfocused on areas that are superfluous to the end goal. I was helping one client move house, only to find out that she was looking for new curtain fabric for her home-to-be even before we had completed the estate agent's forms for selling her old one.

My job was to bring her focus back to the critical steps involved while also giving her licence to visualize those new curtains (this added motivation!).

I believe planning and prioritizing can be a challenge for many people because they are tools needed for the future, and the future can feel even more overwhelming than the present does.

It is definitely worth eliciting the support of a colleague to help with planning and prioritizing as we often cannot see what needs to be done first. Professional organizers can help, and it is of no surprise that there is a wealth of project management tools and resources to help. Often used is the SMART technique to support the task in hand:

- **S** – Specific
- **M** – Measurable
- **A** – Achievable
- **R** – Realistic
- **T** – Timely

Start by formulating a precise goal, then set a deadline, make an achievable and realistic plan to reach that deadline, and include time scales for each part. Good research throughout is vital. The use of a planning template can be effective. My boss in the project management team I worked in insisted on a 'clear desk policy', which meant we could only have one piece of paper on our desk at any given time, as he believed this helped with staying on-task.

Set a reminder to review your plan and priorities. This can be weekly and does not need to be too arduous. Bullet-point your plans and priorities. Also, learn to say 'no' to other people's demands. Learning to say 'no' is actually saying 'yes' to yourself. Remind yourself that you are working towards your priorities, not anyone else's.

Planning for the day, the week or month ahead can give a real sense of control. This can apply to meal planning, shopping, writing a book, going to the gym, when we have our meals, when we pay our rent, when we put our rubbish out, and so on. Planning and prioritizing aren't necessarily only about long-term goals but also short-term ones.

7 Organization

Other words for organization include order, meticulousness, systematicness, precision and efficiency. It is about the capacity to set up routines and systems that can be followed, to find a place for everything and to keep things in their place. Organizational skills very much rely on the other executive skills such as planning and prioritizing, decision making and focus, among others. Are we born organized? No, of course not, and I think organization can certainly be learned. It is so very easy to become disorganized if things get out of kilter. Organization requires information and materials, schedules, routine and ... repeat, repeat, repeat. It's finding a system that works for you. Having less stuff in your home as well as in your head certainly helps with establishing organization.

I have one client who needs to make some big decisions about whether to downsize or, as she says, 'right-size'. With a home full of years of memories, unwanted gifts, incomplete projects, hopes and missed opportunities, she is finding it difficult to decide. We are organizing her head and her home to allow headspace for her to think and breathe.

If you are naturally organized, you probably have a neat and tidy environment, have a system for everything, are able to maintain those systems, dislike clutter, unpack straight away on returning from a trip, put the shopping away immediately, never run out of essential items and pay bills on time. You will probably recognize that our external environment is a manifestation of our internal environment.

If you struggle in this area, you probably always forget something when you pack your bag for a holiday, have lots of clutter around the home, struggle to find places for things, fail to put things away, find it difficult to maintain any kind of system, lose keys and phones, run out of toilet rolls and put off emptying the washing machine. You likely complain bitterly if someone else moves something that you have not put away.

8 Stress tolerance

Stress tolerance is the capacity to not only manage things well in ordinary times but also to thrive in stressful and pressurized situations which might involve change, uncertainty and rapid decision making. Such people likely crave stimulation, excitement and sensation and will enjoy windsurfing over watching a film. Stress tolerance is about being good in a crisis and being able to deal with the unexpected.

It tends to be that people who are challenged by stress tolerance may well be low on cognitive flexibility. There are also overlaps here with emotional regulation. If you are challenged by stress tolerance, you may prefer routine and not relish change or when things don't pan out in the way you had hoped.

Ask for help if you are stress intolerant, build in recovery time and downtime, and use your home as a haven. Set aside regular time to help manage stress. Exercise regularly, and avoid sugar and caffeine.

9 Time management

This refers to the ability to realistically estimate and measure how long things will take to do. Time blindness can impede staying aware of the time, seeing it and planning it. Many people find it difficult to measure time, miscalculate how long something will take to do, and try to cram in too much. For those who can manage effectively, time gives a real sense of control.

If this is a function you have trouble with, you may find it difficult to measure how long something will take, pack too many things in and be overoptimistic about how time can expand to meet your needs. On the other hand, you may struggle with meeting deadlines and not necessarily be punctual, and always think there is never enough time.

If we are challenged by time, we are often in the 'now' – not being able to see the future and plan for it. Many people challenged with chronic disorganization struggle with time management, and this can be connected to ADHD, depression and OCD, among other conditions.

One of the most frequent complaints I hear is 'I don't have enough time'. I also often hear, 'Sorry I'm late, I couldn't find my car keys ...' 'Sorry my rent is late, I couldn't find a card machine ...' Chronic disorganization is often linked with poor time management. Many of us feel we are time poor, and without enough time we become chronically disorganized.

Sometimes it is also about how we spend our time and realizing that scrolling on our phone first thing after we wake up can absorb half an hour of our time. What else could you be doing during those 30 minutes? Being conscious of our 'life minutes' can be illuminating. Remember: being in control of your time and learning to say no to things that do not feel right is saying yes to ourselves and providing ourselves with a choice about how we spend our time.

10 Cognitive flexibility

Cognitive flexibility, also known as flexible thinking, is the ability to adjust to different situations and circumstances. It's about being able to 'change sails', adapt and adjust to a new way of thinking and go with the flow, especially when schedules and planning events are changed unexpectedly and at the last minute. It helps us deal with uncertainty and manage our emotions when things aren't going to plan. Some of us find it difficult to quickly adapt and respond to sudden and new situations. Flexible thinking means being able to formulate and resort to 'plan B'.

Individuals with inflexible and rigid thinking often become set in rigid routines, slavishly follow rules and rituals, and quite often have repetitive sets of behaviours. A desire for sameness and order often co-occur.

For those of you who struggle with this function, you may not easily adjust to the unexpected and feel overwhelmingly discombobulated at a change of plan. You may find it difficult to adjust to a plan B, and find it hard when things go off course, whether that's a late bus, the corner shop running out of your favourite ice cream, a change in venue, or the cancellation of a plan. Quite often, there may be a freeze response if things happen that have not been anticipated or foreseen.

Cognitive flexibility is something we have all had to adapt to in recent years because of the COVID-19 pandemic and the shifting rules around restrictions. Having a plan B or learning to adapt to ever-changing situations requires coping strategies so we can adjust easily and effectively. We need time to process the changes, time to breathe and recognize that there are situations we cannot control. A flexible mindset and emotional agility take time to develop. Take a break or time out, go for a walk or take a nap and you will often feel a shift in your mindset. Exercise works wonders and creates a great mental boost as does sleep. Talking things through can often be reassuring, too.

Change your routine and step outside your comfort zone: try wearing odd socks or cooking a new recipe; take a different route to work or try a new means of transport. Change the context and you will feel your mind shift. Try being spontaneous – try a new flavour of tea; turn left instead of right on your dog walk.

Recognize your mindset and learn to 'bend' it. These techniques will help you face up to the most challenging of goals and aims you must confront.

11 Goal perseverance

This refers to the ability to set goals and build in the relevant steps to be able to pursue these goals, making a plan around them, identifying where to start and putting in a timeline (see the SMART goals explained above). It is also having the ability to complete a goal despite distractions.

Who doesn't love a goal? Especially when it comes to how we want our homes to work for us and how we want to feel about ourselves. Goal setting – and seeing others succeed at achieving their goals – inspires motivation. Many of us have goals and are goal-oriented but may fail to understand what needs to be put in place to achieve them – the start, the middle and the end and the details about every stage.

Goals need to be rewarding, beneficial and of positive consequence, staying true to what is tangible and realistic and harmonious to other goals. A goal needs to be *good enough*. If this is a challenge for you, you may struggle to set effective goals, be happy with where you are and not feel the need to strive for goals.

Goal focus is often a strength for neurodivergent individuals and can be used to support challenges and weaknesses in other areas including organization, planning and prioritizing, and sense of time. Being goal focused means you can set long-term goals and pursue them, complete goals despite obstacles, and be able to get back on track if distracted.

Have your goal visible on paper, computer screen or phone to remind you what you're focusing on, and work backwards from the completion: What step comes just before completion? What is the step before that? And so on. Ask yourself what you need at each stage to complete it. Make a list of what you need before you start and get that ready in advance.

Again, vocalize your goals to a friend or mentor. Look at the obstacles, scope the goal and break it down into sizeable chunks.

The Eisenhower box

The Eisenhower box, which is also known as the Eisenhower matrix, was named after President Dwight Eisenhower (1890–1969) – the 34th president of the USA. His methods of task management, time management and productivity have been widely studied, and the 'Eisenhower box' he himself developed is a good decision-making tool which helps you decide on what is important and how you can organize your activities, priorities and actions, and helps focus on productivity and effectiveness. It can be used for specific daily tasks but also as a weekly/monthly planner and can include broader goals and wishes.

The tasks in the box break down as follows:

- Urgent and important (tasks you will do immediately)
- Important, but not urgent (tasks you will schedule to do later)
- Urgent, but not important (tasks you will delegate to someone else)
- Neither urgent nor important (tasks that you will eliminate).

Practise using this strategy yourself, using pen and paper. Over time, the categorization of tasks will become second nature.

EISENHOWER BOX

	URGENT	NOT URGENT
IMPORTANT	DO TASKS THAT ARE BOTH IMPORTANT AND URGENT	SCHEDULE TASKS THAT ARE IMPORTANT BUT NOT URGENT
NOT IMPORTANT	DELEGATE TASKS THAT ARE NOT IMPORTANT BUT ARE URGENT	ELIMINATE TASKS THAT ARE NOT IMPORTANT AND NOT URGENT

12 Self-awareness

Being self-aware means having the ability to step back and view yourself in a situation and having the capacity to reflect on your thoughts and actions. It may be that you 'cannot see the wood for the trees', and view things rationally. This function is also referred to as self-monitoring or metacognition. It's the ability to see our shortcomings and identify what we need to do differently.

If this is a function that is not a challenge, you may see other points of view, easily reflect and see the bigger picture and how it all fits in. You may see more than one point of view, be able to reflect constructively on your thoughts and actions, and see how everything fits together. You are, in other words, able to see the wood for the trees and able to stand back and look in.

In order to look at the bigger picture, we need to let go of the detail and not sweat the small stuff. We need to look up, not down and ask ourselves what we are wanting to achieve. Bullet-point the actions needed and then chunk them down. Mind-mapping can be helpful, as can committing time to think, to reflect and keep vocalizing what it is you are wanting to achieve.

When something is distressing us, we're so close to it, involved with it, part of it, that it's really hard to stand back from what's happening. We see the close-up view, but we can't see anything else. If we could zoom out our view, like a helicopter hovering above, we'd be able to see the bigger picture, other viewpoints and positive aspects, and discover alternative approaches to a situation. We could stand back, be less emotionally involved and see a different perspective.

Sometimes when I get bogged down with negative thoughts and react to situations disproportionately, I remind myself to be grateful that I have petrol in the car, a warm bed to sleep in, I am not hungry and I am not thirsty. Spend some time each day practising this strategy and be aware of what we do by default as a habit.

Satnav is my best friend

I consider myself to be fairly neurotypical and am fairly even across the board of executive functioning, but my inability to follow directions is shocking and this is linked to my working memory.

It has become a joke in the family that both my daughter and I are geographically dyslexic. I think another term for it is 'directional dyslexia'. My mother was the same. When I was a child, my family spent Sunday afternoons 'going for a drive'. I dreaded those drives as my parents would always argue due to the fact that, while my father drove, my mother had to provide directions by trying to follow a map – which she always failed to do. I, too, cannot follow a map, I do not know my east from my west, and have been known to drive around London's circular M25 in the 'wrong' direction (that is, take the long route round to a destination).

And then satellite navigation – satnav – was invented. My goodness, it was lifesaving. My satnav is called Sean, who speaks with an Irish accent (which I love) and tells me exactly where to go. To me this is my biggest aid and support. One day when my car had broken down and my daughter and I were waiting for the recovery service, we discovered that we could change the voice on the satnav and spent the time learning accents.

I recently went to hospital for a routine cancer screening and the receptionist gave me quite a lengthy set of directions to follow to the mobile unit. Previously, I would had have a meltdown and become quite tearful, knowing that I would get lost en route. This time I calmly told the receptionist that I had directional dyslexia, and she asked a cleaner who was on her way to the unit to guide me there. I now feel no shame and am not embarrassed, nor do I consider myself stupid.

Interestingly, the same dyslexia also applies not only to reading a map but also being able to understand a floor plan. My daughter, Sasha, was moving house and her partner drew a floor plan of their bedroom to show how they might arrange the furniture. He thought he was being really helpful, but my daughter could not understand it and glazed over. It is a symptom of dyslexia. I am the same – when my clients show me floor plans of their new extensions, I cannot read them. I know it is a genuine condition, as does my daughter, so I have stopped beating myself up about it.

Emotional intelligence

The definition of emotional intelligence is: 'The ability to monitor one's own and others' feelings and emotions, to discriminate among them and to use this information to guide one's thinking and actions.' (Salovey & Mayer (1990) as quoted by O'Conner, Hill, Kaya & Martin (2019)). There are five key elements to emotional intelligence (EI):

- self-awareness
- self-regulation
- motivation
- empathy
- social skills.

For people who have high levels of EI, they are able to recognize their strengths to help overcome their challenges.

For more information on EI, please see Daniel Coleman's book *Emotional Intelligence* (Bantam, 1995).

Executive dysfunction

Executive dysfunction can be hereditary, be related to a condition such as autism, or acquired through trauma or post-traumatic stress disorder (PTSD), dementia, a stroke, ageing or traumatic brain injury. It is most commonly people with ADHD and other neurological conditions who are challenged with executive dysfunction, but in times of stress, fatigue and uncertainty we can all experience deficits in executive functioning. We can all be prone to forgetting where we last put our phone, our wallet and our keys. There are a whole raft of reasons why our executive functions can be dulled. Stress, fatigue, diet and hormones can all contribute. We all feel at times that we 'can't get our act together'.

Sharon Morein is an associate professor at Anglia Ruskin University, Cambridge, UK, and the chair of the ARU Possessions and Hoarding Collective, 'a group of academics and professionals who aim to improve understanding of how people interact with their possessions'.[4] Her research integrates psychology, cognitive neuroscience and psychiatry to better understand mental health conditions such as hoarding, ADHD and OCD.

Traits and state

Traits such as clutter or excessive attachment to possessions can vary from person to person. Some people like to think that our traits place us somewhere along a continuum – from being wonderful and perfect at one extreme to suffering from an extreme case of hoarding disorder on the other. But where do you draw the line for any given person and when would you need intervention? People are more complicated than that, and where you find yourself along the continuum is time and circumstances dependent. Our state and not just our traits matter and they can interact. Everyone can have a good day (moving towards the more wonderful end of things) or a bad day (moving in the other direction). There are also circumstances in our lives that can shift us along the line – for example, if we have just moved to a new place or

---

[4] See https://www.aru.ac.uk/science-and-engineering/research/institutes-and-groups/the-aru-possessions-and-hoarding-collective

have a baby or a toddler in the house. Or, conversely, won the lottery and hired a full-time personal assistant!

Two key aspects are, first, whether the situation is distressing and impairing, and second, if it is hampering the ability of someone in the household to carry out their everyday activities (work, socializing or maintaining a safe environment) for a prolonged period of time. In both these situations it's time to take note and take action.

If we think about clutter, one can consider the cognitive functions that can contribute – namely our control functions, such as our ability to plan, prioritize, make decisions and reduce distractibility (there are so many more!). Control functions do not work in isolation; they interact with our emotional state. If we are upset, haven't slept well or are dealing with stressful things, it is difficult to engage our control functions productively. Conversely, if we are struggling with organizing things, or having to make decisions and adjust to changes, we can find ourself stressed and unhappy. The everyday pressures of life place demands on our time and energy and we have only so much 'mental bandwidth' (see below). When this is squeezed, such as when going through a rough patch, we can find not only our emotional state but also our control functions under pressure and it can become that much harder to remember things, prioritize and get over any tendencies to procrastinate.

Bandwidth

Squeezes on our control functions can happen gradually and sneak up on us, even in response to clear events. It can take time to appreciate that this has been happening. Take, for example, the case of a woman who told me she had been experiencing difficulties managing her husband's clutter. She had always done this routinely, but in the last few years it was so much more difficult and things were getting on top of her and she couldn't figure out why it had become so much more challenging. After all, he hadn't changed. It turned out that a few years before she had suffered a brain injury from a fall. Although she had made a full recovery, since the injury it had become gradually more difficult to manage her husband's clutter and excessive saving tendencies. Together we came to the realization that her difficulties with managing the clutter in the house resulted from her mental bandwidth having become a bit narrower. This hadn't occurred to her beforehand and helped her understand how her situation had changed. Now that she appreciated where the source of her new difficulties lay, she could adopt a few strategies to help her – for example, setting a regular alarm on her phone on the weekend to tell her to devote 20 minutes to organizing and even discarding some of the new items her husband had brought into the house. The alarm helped remove the need to remember and plan this and to have the perseverance to do it regularly. The timing of the alarm coincided with when she would likely be in the house, feeling relaxed and rested.

Factors and functions

Control functions do not work in isolation, but interact with our emotional state. If we are upset, haven't slept well and are dealing with stressful things, it is difficult to engage our control functions productively. Conversely, if we are struggling with organizing things, having to make decisions and adjust to changes we can find ourself stressed and unhappy. The everyday pressures of life place demands on our time and energy and we have only so much 'mental bandwidth'. When this is squeezed, such as when we are going through a rough patch, we can find not only our emotional state but also our control functions under pressure and it can become that much harder to remember things, prioritize and get over any tendencies to procrastinate.

Many people who struggle with too much clutter, such as those who hoard, have long reported feeling they have undiagnosed ADHD and in fact there is some research to support a link between the two. This is not surprising as problems with control functions are a key characteristic of many individuals with ADHD (although not all of them), where they fall under the umbrella label of 'inattention'. When you are that much more distractable, it is easy to see how your living spaces can get cluttered without you meaning for it to happen. After all, if you tend to procrastinate, then unpleasant chores, such as dealing with the post, are going to lead to piles of stuff, which in turn require more and more energy and bandwidth to address. It is therefore not surprising that DOOM ('didn't organize, only moved') piles have been associated with ADHD on social media. In fact, being forgetful can also mean that it might seem like a good idea to have things placed where they can easily be seen, contributing to more clutter.

People with ADHD can struggle with change, so making decisions to clear out and throw away possessions that have been around for years will prove all the more challenging. Individuals with ADHD can sometimes struggle with thinking things through fully, and when this is coupled with forgetfulness and existing clutter, it can easily result in their acquiring even more, thus intensifying the problem further. For example, they go out to buy cat food because they fail to recall that their flatmate has told them they have already picked up some the day before. While clutter can lead to a sense of being overwhelmed cognitively (e.g. visual overload), those with ADHD are all the more susceptible to this, shrinking their 'bandwidth' even more, contributing to a kind of cycle.

Nutrition and executive functioning

What we put in our bodies can really affect our executive functioning. Our physical health and our mental health both feed into each other and I recognize that nutrition plays a huge part in our sense of wellbeing more generally. I can always tell if my clients have not eaten breakfast, are charged on too much caffeine and more distracted that usual. Processed foods are a huge contributor to not being able to focus, function and follow through. I recently had a rock cake for breakfast and had to spend the whole day finding ways of diluting the head rush it gave me. I cannot tolerate any foods with MSG – it gives me the equivalent feeling of a hangover.

Fellow organizer and coach Kate Wren shares her tips on helping with focus, energy and concentration. She recommends POWERFUL:

- P *Protein-rich diet* to support balanced blood sugar. Well-balanced blood sugar is very important for brain health, mood, concentration and energy. In contrast, unstable blood sugar can lead to irritability, brain fog, anxiety, poor sleep and low energy.
- O *Oily foods rich in omega 3*, such as fish, avocado, walnuts and eggs help our brains function well so that we can think and focus.

- **W** *Water* is so important to health. Dehydration impairs brain function, causing inattention and impairment of short-term memory. Drinking water regularly through the day and avoiding dehydrating drinks such as those containing caffeine, sugar and alcohol helps our brains to function optimally.
- **E** *EPA/DHA* found in fish oils (there are also vegan sources of EPA). Omega 3 oils are so important for brain health that it deserves another mention. As well as including oily foods in diet, when concentration, motivation, focus, mood or seasonal affected disorder (SAD) are experienced, taking concentrated doses of fish oils can be a very helpful addition to the diet.
- **R** *Rich in vegetables.* Vegetables and fruits that are rich in vitamins A, C and E, such as broccoli, leafy green vegetables, tomatoes and berries are rich in antioxidants. Eating them helps brain function by increasing blood flow to the brain and reducing inflammation.
- **F** *Flavourful.* Healthy eating doesn't mean compromising on flavour. Make sure that what you eat is a treat for your senses.
- **U** *Unprocessed.* A great way to move to a healthier diet is to avoid ultra-processed foods. It has been found that the ability to learn, remember, reason and solve problems is worse in people who eat ultra-processed foods than those who eat whole foods.
- **L** *Less sugar and sweeteners.* As well as including protein in the diet, it is important to avoid foods which are high in sugar or sweeteners so that we get the benefits of stable blood sugar such as better energy, more balanced mood and better concentration. It doesn't take long after reducing the sugar we eat before we start to notice how naturally sweet unprocessed foods like fruit and some vegetables are.

When we feel physically fit, our brain and minds can respond so much easier to the challenges of daily life. Sleep, exercise, relaxation and a healthy diet can impact on so much of how we function. Sleep deprivation can certainly impact on poor decision making, unhealthy foods packed with chemicals can contribute to an inability to stay focused, and lack of exercise and relaxation will certainly make us feel sluggish and unmotivated.

Gut health is so important, too. I know that a friend of mine who struggles with organization recently looked at gut health and mentioned to me that since she has been looking after her gut, her focus has improved significantly. She talks about only having two radios on in her head, as opposed to twenty!

Neurotransmitters and hormones

These, too, play a crucial role in executive functioning. Our ability to be organized, keep focus and see projects through is dependent on how well our body is maintaining these all-important chemicals. If we can find ways of boosting the wellbeing of our brain and improving the way that we feel, then this in turn helps us function and tackle the challenges and demands on our day to day life. We can focus that much better, have more energy, more positivity, and greater cognitive capacity and motivation. We need a cocktail of different strategies and having an awareness of how chemicals and hormones impact us can be hugely beneficial.

Dopamine

Dopamine is a chemical found naturally in the human body. It is a neurotransmitter, meaning it sends signals from the body to the brain. Dopamine plays a part in controlling the movements a person makes, as well as their emotional responses. The right balance of dopamine is vital for both physical and mental wellbeing.

Different levels of dopamine can contribute to motivation and our ability to complete a task, and it is responsible, too, for time management and time estimation. It has been suggested that, when there are low levels of dopamine, time perception can be distorted. Activities such as eating, engaging in self-care activities, tidying a sock drawer and celebrating little achievements can all increase levels of dopamine.

Foods that contribute to higher levels of dopamine include protein-based foods, salmon, mackerel, almonds, walnuts, fruit and vegetables. It is present especially in bananas and dark chocolate.

Serotonin

Serotonin is the key hormone that stabilizes our mood and provides us with feelings of wellbeing and happiness. This hormone impacts your entire body. It enables brain cells and other nervous system cells to communicate with each other.

Serotonin is known as the mood stabilizer. It is a neurotransmitter that helps soothe the brain. Activities such as meditating, running, walking in nature, swimming and cycling all increase levels of serotonin. It helps decrease our worries and concerns with mood regulation. Foods that boost serotonin include cheese, eggs, salmon, nuts, seeds and tofu.

Oxytocin

Oxytocin helps regulate our emotional responses and pro-social behaviours, including trust, empathy, positive memories, processing of bonding cues and positive communication. Activities including cooking for someone, cuddles, sex, massage (either giving one or receiving one), holding hands, stroking a dog or cat and listening to music all increase our levels of oxytocin. Foods to boost oxytocin are those high in vitamins C and D and include mushrooms, peppers, figs and avocados.

Endorphins

Endorphins interact with the opiate receptors in the brain to reduce our perception of pain and act similarly to drugs such as morphine and codeine. Stress and pain are the most common factors leading to the release of endorphins. Endorphins release a positive feeling in the body, similar to that feeling that follows a workout often described as a 'runner's high'. Endorphins provide an energizing, positive sense of being. Activities that release endorphins include dancing, random acts of kindness, laughter, any exercise, essential oils and watching comedy.

Top advice from ADHD specialist Sarah Bickers

Sarah Bickers is an ADHD specialist, ICF coach, professional organizer, ADHD speaker and trainer. Here she shares her tips on her work with helping those with executive functioning:

When tackling executive function challenges, by far the most useful strategy I've found for both myself and my clients is to be kinder to ourselves.

Ironically, while we're beating ourselves up for those everyday mistakes, we're not actually helping ourselves solve the problem. Our thinking brain analyses what is or isn't working – and also helps us get stuff done. But as soon as we feel judged, whether by others, or even by our own inner critical voice, our THINKING shifts to FEELING. Those feelings of shame or hopelessness divert us into our more primitive, emotional brain, trapping us in a downwards spiral and stopping us learning from our mistakes.

Imagine this scenario:

I have an appointment to go shopping with my friend Tamara and I am late. I'm on the bus feeling stressed but am deluding myself I could still get there in time. By the time I arrive Tamara has been waiting for 45 minutes and is visibly fed up. I apologize defensively, making excuses and even lying about the bus being late. But I've been late before with Tamara, and our time together is ruined. She says: 'If you really cared about me, you wouldn't keep being late.'

On the way home, shame's judgemental voice continues taunting me: 'Why was I late again? I'm always late! Tamara's right, I'm a bad friend. If I cared about her, of course I would have been on time! I'm so rubbish at timekeeping.'

How do we get past such powerful feelings which keep us stuck in these destructive behaviours?

To tackle any executive function challenge, we need first to recognize what's going on so we can exit that emotional spiral. We need to challenge that inner critic and start being kinder to ourselves. There's a powerful tool we can use here, to help us find our way back to problem solving – it's curiosity. As ADHD coach Jeff Copper says: 'Observe but don't judge.'

Let's revisit the above situation; this time choosing to be kinder, and using curiosity instead of judgement. (This isn't letting me off the hook – using this tool to *notice* what's happening allows the option of change.)

Back on the bus, but this time ...

'Wow, that was stressful, I'm definitely going to be late. I'd better call Tamara so she can decide what to do.'

(Here I'm being honest with myself and communicating with Tamara to manage her expectations. Perhaps she can get a coffee while she's waiting?)

'Why was I so late leaving today? What can I learn from this for next time?'

Here's a few possibilities to think about:

- *I tried to squeeze 'just one more job' in before I left. And I lost track of time: perhaps I could set an alarm for 10 minutes before I need to leave? Or I could put an analogue clock in the bathroom so I can see the time better?*
- *I was late because I couldn't find my keys. Perhaps I could put a basket in the hallway for my keys?*
- *I had to run back home because I forgot my phone. Perhaps I could take a moment for a final check – or keep a checklist by the door?*

I think this example demonstrates that curiosity beats judgement every time:

Judgement looks backwards and says we'll never change; it traps us in that spiral of negative emotions, focused on our mistakes.

Curiosity, by contrast, allows us to make small incremental changes, at our own pace. Yes, we may always find some things challenging, but becoming kinder to ourselves and getting curious about how we work best often makes us happier, as well as helping us move forward.

Five takeaways

1 Acknowledging the drivers for our behaviours is useful, as is knowing that we use distractions to detract from discomfort.
2 Learning to control our emotions is a real strength, and the ability to acknowledge difficult thoughts and feelings rather than avoid them is a skill.
3 Procrastination and perfectionism go hand in hand. Remember: 'Done is better than perfect.'
4 Change your routine and step outside your comfort zone.
5 Curiosity about your CD beats judgement every time: Judgement looks backwards and says we'll never change; curiosity allows us to make small incremental changes, at our own pace.

4

Hoarding

The definition of hoarding, according to *DSM-5*, is 'persistent difficulty discarding or parting with possessions, regardless of their actual value'. 'This difficulty', the definition continues, 'is due to a perceived need to save the items, and to the distress associated with discarding them. The difficulty of discarding possessions results in the accumulation of possessions that congest and clutter active living areas. [...] The hoarding causes clinically significant distress or impairment to social, occupational or other important areas of functioning.'

Hoarding used to be recognized only as a symptom of obsessive compulsive disorder (OCD). However, in 2018, the World Health Organization recognized hoarding disorder in its own right with the publication of *The International Classification of Diseases*. Many hoarders exhibit the same level of anxiety, compulsions and anxiety issues as those affected by OCD.

Chronic disorganization versus hoarding

Hoarding, as we said earlier, can be defined as when a person feels distress at the thought of getting rid of items. With chronic disorganization, by contrast, there is no emotional attachment to the items, only an impaired ability to sort them. The home may well present as 'hoarded' but the clutter is a result of challenges to executive functions such as the ability to organize, focus, categorize and allocate time to sorting possessions, as well as to impulse control and working memory.

Often, people ask me, 'Do you think I'm a hoarder?' First, I will say that there is so much stereotyping and stigma connected to the word 'hoarder' that it can be really brave for someone to use that word. Someone from one of my hoarding support groups piped up in one session, 'I am not a hoarder, I am just hoardacious.' Hoarding, I want to stress, should be defined as when a person feels distress at the thought of getting rid of items.

The 'hoarded home'

The conditions of hoarders' homes are quite often challenging. Not all are squalid and dirty, but many are, with very little access to hot water and heating. There may be no working sink to wash up in or functioning bath or shower, let alone a bed to sleep in or cooker to heat up food. Toilets are often blocked, with damp and mould prevalent. Some homes trap bad smells; others are deep in dust through the sheer volume of paperwork and books, while the smell of rotting food, urine and cat faeces can be overwhelming. With limited access to open windows, air within a hoarded home is often stagnant and polluted.

Hoarding manifests itself in multiple forms, from the hoarding of yoghurt pots or unusual-sized cereal boxes to books and newspapers, animals, electrical items, food and, more recently, digital items.

At the extreme is the hoarding of substances produced by bodily functions – a phenomenon referred to by environmental health personnel as 'wet hoarding'. I have occasionally seen houses where urine has been stored away in jars or milk bottles, used so the person did not have to get up and go to the toilet in the middle of the night.

The implications and impact of hoarding are vast and present a range of health and safety problems, including the risk of fire. Research suggests that 30 per cent of accidental deaths in domestic fires involve hoarding. The challenges presented by hoarded homes can include difficulties in gaining access to gas and electricity, restricted entry and exit access, water leaks, mould, and pest, flea and rat infestations.

Additionally, there are financial implications for those with hoarding tendencies and/or chronic disorganization. They may not have access to their paperwork or know where it is. Money is spent on replacing duplicates not only of important documents but also lost keys and mobile phones. Unpaid bills may incur costs. If environmental health officers are involved in clearing a house, the costs relating to a forced clear-out are charged to the homeowner and a further charge made on the house. Financial pressures are also presented by hoarders who have a compulsive need to shop.

Adults who exhibit hoarding behaviours often have powerful reasons for holding on to their acquisitions, whether for sentimental reasons, for their beauty and/or aesthetic value, their actual or imputed usefulness ('It might come in handy one day'), their emotional connection to an event or person, their monetary value or for associated memories. Hoarders' reasons for not discarding items are varied and include variations on:

- 'It would be wasteful to throw it away.'
- 'It cost money so I need to keep it.'
- 'It was a gift.'
- 'I will miss it.'
- 'I will forget that I ever had it.'
- 'It is part of my history/my present, and it may provide me with an opportunity in the future.'

Hoarding can be triggered by a severe trauma, bereavement, a sense of loss, grief or poverty. Additionally, redundancy, low self-esteem and a lack of nurturing and/or love felt as a child can trigger hoarding behaviours. Sometimes hoarding behaviours can develop through the influence of parents, or be learned. Some people with hoarding difficulties may suppress their psychological pain by hoarding. Confronting, recognizing and reconciling with traumas and other emotional issues can often be difficult, so hoarding can be seen as a solution to a problem.

Hoarding can also be connected with neurodivergence, and more research is being done to look at the relationship between ADHD and hoarding.

Hoarding is not just a private concern. Hoarding affects the whole family: children, wives, husbands and parents, as well as best friends, pets, neighbours and the wider community. Family members may experience embarrassment, shame and guilt relating to the person with hoarding issues. Hoarding can have a significant impact on family life; there may be increased tension and resentment towards the hoarder. Hoarding can mean children are unable to have friends around to visit or stay over. Family traditions and rituals can be compromised: it may not be possible to eat at the table together, or to invite extended family over at Christmas. In severe cases where living space is lost due to hoarding, homework cannot be done and sleep can be disturbed as children have to share beds. Relations with spouses and other family members can be strained.

There are various reasons why people hoard. Hoarding expert Dr Gail Steketee of Boston University, co-author with psychologist Dr Randy Frost of several books including *Stuff: Compulsive Hoarding and the Meaning of Things*, says that there can be a number of contributing factors, including:

- being brought up in a chaotic or confusing home, or moving frequently
- cognitive issues that affect decision making and problem solving
- attention deficit disorder
- anxiety and/or depression
- excessive guilt about waste
- genetics and family history, given that hoarding behaviours often tend to run in families.

It's well documented that hoarding tendencies can be triggered by certain life events. Research indicates that trauma, as well as learned behaviour from being raised in a 'hoarded home', can contribute to hoarding tendencies. The death of a loved one, divorce, eviction or losing one's possessions in a fire can all contribute to the disorder, according to researchers at the Mayo Clinic, the medical research group based in Rochester, Minnesota. Dr Jessica Grisham of the University of New South Wales found that the link between hoarding behaviours and traumatic events, such as losing a partner or child, is especially important when people develop hoarding tendencies in later life, particularly when it follows soon after the loss. For others, hoarding can be a way of coping with an emotional upset, and can act as a form of emotional insulation.

People also hoard because of perfectionism. Perfectionists generally procrastinate through fear of making the wrong decision, which leads to indecision and keeping everything 'just in case', the result of which is clutter (see Chapter 3).

Hoarding issues can be triggered by deprivation – by 'not having a lot' when growing up, or from having had a frugal childhood in which nothing was ever thrown away. People with such childhoods consequently make up for this later on in life as a substitute for the feeling of having been denied books, toys, clothes, even friendships. Lack of meaningful relationships can trigger hoarding, which in turn leads to social isolation, the items concerned taking on a heightened importance in a person's life to fill a void and act as a replacement for interpersonal relationships.

Overcome Compulsive Hoarding with That Hoarder is an excellent podcast series produced by someone who has hoarding behaviours but who wishes to remain anonymous (https://www.overcomecompulsivehoarding.co.uk/category/podcast/). On one of her podcasts, she gives this advice:

> *You might wish that you could make use of your grandparents' cabinet, but you can't. That's OK. That's OK. Your home doesn't exist to hold on to the ghosts of everyone you ever met, every dream you ever had or every purchase you ever made. To quote Elsa [from* Frozen*], 'Let it go.' It might be uncomfortable, it's difficult, but you can't save everything.*

Some people hoard for aesthetic and artistic reasons – because they appreciate and find real joy in the way objects look, or in their colour, shape, the way an ornament might reflect in certain light, the texture and feel. Objects for artists can take on a complex meaning and can be hoarded for the furthering of their art. You are probably familiar with art exhibitions in which artists have used objects to represent their artistic self – from unmade beds to crisp packets and tins of baked beans. In some instances, it is perhaps not too much of a stretch to see the hoarded home as a kind of extended artwork, created by the hoarder as a way of giving meaning to their life.

People also hoard for sentimental reasons, to help recapture a time when life felt good and secure. We worked in one woman's home which for her represented happier times in the 1970s, and the flat was stuck in that era, a kind of time capsule. It was as if time stood still for her after that decade, which was when her husband passed away.

Control

Having and feeling a lack of control seems to be a recurring theme in relation to hoarding. Hoarding provides control as well as a sense of security and a feeling of safety for many people with hoarding difficulties. It acts as a protective shield, a form of insulation, a cave. If people feel their safety is being threatened, this can provoke a real need to control their possessions, which is why it is important to consult with any individual you are trying to help before even touching anything.

I worked with one woman whose very complicated life was further compounded by breast cancer, as a result of which she had undergone a double mastectomy. This was just one aspect of her life over which she had no control. She now recognizes that her hoarding implies an attempt to assert control over her life, and she is working towards knowing what she can control and what she cannot, and accepting that she cannot control everything.

Types of hoarding

There are commonly four established types of hoarding: sentimental, instrumental, intrinsic and recycling. To these I have added a fifth and sixth – eco-hoarding and fact hoarding.

Sentimental hoarding

I think most of us can relate to finding it difficult to let go of sentimental items. Each item we keep reminds us of special events in our lives, and items associated with loved ones who are no longer with us are especially difficult to let go of. We hoard our memories, our timeline and our history. In our grief and sadness, we cling on to the precious memories which are often held in objects. There can be a real sense of dishonour and guilt when we discard items. I remind clients that our loved ones would not want us to be beholden to these items. We can keep our memories in our hearts and not in our homes. For some people, homes become storage units of loved ones' possessions or even shrines in their memory.

Instrumental hoarding

Instrumental hoarding (or 'just in case' hoarding) is very common, and I think most of us can relate to this; it's just that those with hoarding issues do it on a much larger scale. Who doesn't have a drawer full of 'odds and ends' and random items? Engineers, teachers and artists I know often have a heightened capacity to see the usefulness of items, and dream up endless possible functions for them. Couldn't those spokes from a broken umbrella be used to clean out drains? Those toilet roll tubes to tidy cables or propagate sweet peas? Those lollipop sticks to label seedlings and adjust wonky, wobbly tables? The irony is that, if we were attempt to find these 'useful' items, chances are we would have difficulty doing so.

Intrinsic hoarding

Intrinsic hoarding involves items being acquired for their aesthetic appeal for their uniqueness and beauty. Intrinsic hoarding, also known as aesthetic hoarding, can be very tactile, sparkly and childlike. I like, I want, I buy. We see the smoothness of the leather, the softness of the cashmere, the grain of the wood and the sweet aroma of the candle. For some it can include a particular shade of purple, an unusual piece of sea glass, the shape of a handkerchief. We can be possessed by a real urge to gather, collect, squirrel away and hoard.

Eco-hoarding

We hate to waste anything, we want to protect our planet, to reuse, repurpose and manage our resources. But this can also be a growing motivation for hoarding, and for some their homes become their own landfill. The sense of responsibility to save everything can feel overwhelming – I once read this pertinent phrase: 'Having the waste of the world on your shoulders.' We feel a sense of responsibility to protect our planet. However, it really is worth knowing what can be recycled as that can be the key to letting things go – if we know an item can be recycled, upcycled or repurposed, we can let it go out into the world again and free our homes of clutter.

Fact hoarding

I wanted to call this section 'information hoarding', but an online search for this term brings up 'withholding of information', which this is not. Some individuals hoard not only their history, their timeline and their to-do lists but also any interesting information relating to the news, local or international, so as to be able to document and recall recent events. This can be wearing. Some time ago, when I asked my father why he kept all the Chinese takeaway menus that came through his letterbox, he said he wanted to compare the price of spare ribs in 1984 versus the cost in 1992!

Almost all of us can probably identify with one or more of these behaviours but we would not be considered hoarders under the *DSM-5* definition. When, then, does hoarding become hoarding? When it negatively impacts someone's life, the life of others and the wider community.

Where do we start?

When we work with people who have a hoarding problem, we always start by talking about their individual frustrations and challenges in their living environment. This then helps determine where, quite literally, we start. So, if you are trying to deal with your own hoarding, decide on the part of your home that would make a real difference to your life. Usually this will be a small space, the least emotional area of the house, one that will provide maximum impact and produce a positive visual effect.

We often start in kitchens, and for one lady simply concentrating on one area of a kitchen table meant that she could use the table to eat her meals at, rather than the tray she had been using. She has made a commitment to protect this space and values the decluttered area – though her husband quite often sees the space as an opportunity to fill it up again as a way of redistributing the clutter! There is as much work to be done in maintaining a clear space as there is in decluttering a space.

A hoarder's poem

This poem is written by someone I've known for a number of years who is well aware of the devastating effects of trauma and how it can contribute to hoarding behaviours. The author is very passionate about the provision of safe help for those who are vulnerable and avoiding unnecessary harm. She speaks from the heart, and I know her words will resonate with many.

I am a winner
I am no beginner
I know how to help myself
I already accept myself
Even if I don't know this
    yet myself
Don't guide me
I'll guide you
Cos quite honestly
You couldn't have a clue
What to do with a
    traumatized stranger
    would you
And if you think you do
Without specialist training
I need to get away from
    you
I know torrential harm
    raining
When you think you can
    help a stranger with no
    explaining
Why are you strategy
    designing
And deciding
What's best how to start

Clueless assertion
Lack of communication
Swift desertion
Irresponsibility promotion
Abandon before commotion
Harm and run

You haven't developed the art
And knowing through
    discussion how to help me
Building feedback
    preventing catastrophe
Misguided with good
    intention
Unaware of the harm from
    lack of preparation
And desertion
With no explanation
Without consent
apply help not relent
Then realize you've
    overspent
Your promises but not
    repent
A mind execution
Delivered without
    hesitation
When you finally get to
    revelation
That you don't know what
    you're doing
And disassociate from any
    destruction

The help you spun
Unravelling the harm for
    years to come
Shame on your
    irresponsibility
Around vulnerability

Consequence should have
prominence
A clear destruction dagger
don't pretend it's
coincidence

Do be picky moody and
choosy
Scrutinize your help
Avoid the next trauma
And collapse and recovery
unwanted drama
Don't offer yourself as bait
to piranha
Help yourself with your
own plan
Rely on you to fall back on
if you can
Be doing your own thing
In case you enter the
wrong ring
Of help again my friend

A constant negotiation
Your ongoing trust not taken
without solid reason
Have someone in your
corner if you can

To be treated reasonably
With disability vulnerability
Respectfully and equally
With protective legislation
rights validity
Annihilate discriminatory
rigidity
But more realistically
Plan in bad help it's rife
Reduce some strife

Or ridiculously blame us
No right to plead
ignorance
Or just cos you offered to
help take halo-reverence

Don't give access to your
precious brain do not
lend
Protect your mind it's divine
Dump them get away let
that help end
Reduce the trauma tower
Take back your power
Don't be a victim
Don't let it take you over
the brim
Armour protect direct
Polite but show your
intellect
A recovery plan should the
worst happen

You're not that isolated if
self-advocacy is ignored
such a threatening
baton

You're worth the effort
though you shouldn't have
to fight
Against constant disability
plight
Never forget
We are capable and
courageous
We are righteous
And fight to save us

Hoarding and values

Often, the possessions we collect are intimately connected to our personal values.[1] They reflect our self-image and our aspirations, and signal to others how we'd like them to see us. However, sometimes excessive accumulation ends up drowning the very values we cherish the most. The story of one of my clients, Andrea, shows this connection very well, and how, in the end, the same values can lead to a solution.

Andrea's collection

Andrea completed a fine arts degree in her youth, but circumstances led to her working for many years in an administrative role for a construction company. She was good at her work but always missed the creative outlet she previously found in her artistic pursuits. Following a period of ill health and a change of management practices at work, Andrea felt unable to cope with the resultant stress and resigned from her job. Feeling depressed and unsure of her next move, she sought psychotherapy.

At that time, she was living alone in a house which she had bought as a 'doer-upper' many years previously. Planning to do the renovations herself, Andrea had begun collecting magazines and books on design. She also clipped out articles with design ideas from general newspapers and from the advertising flyers which regularly filled her letterbox. At the same time, she kept a lookout for fabric swatches, paint samples, door handles, ornaments and utensils. She was discerning about what she bought, only acquiring things which she thought were aesthetically pleasing. However, over time her home filled up with magazines, samples and belongings, to the point where she found it difficult to find space in her living area and kitchen. Her solution was to purchase an old shipping container, which she stored on a rural property owned by some relatives. Every month or so, Andrea would fill her car with some of the materials she had collected and drive out to the container to deposit them there, but her house would soon fill up again with newly acquired magazines, samples and objects.

Andrea was aware that her home was becoming increasingly neglected, and she felt unhappy about it, saying that to her eyes it was an 'ugly' place to live. Her oppressive surroundings exacerbated her depression and reduced her motivation to organize her

---

[1] Jane Scott, a senior lecturer in clinical psychology at Anglia Ruskin University, Cambridge, UK, has done ground-breaking work in the area of hoarding and values, and I am indebted to her insights in this section.

belongings. She also felt increasingly stressed by her awareness that spending so much time accumulating magazines allowed her no time to read them. She realized, too, that over the years fashions had changed so that much of the content of the design magazines was now out of date, though she worried that hidden in one of the magazines would be the one perfect idea which would transform her dreary surroundings into the exquisitely beautiful home she longed for. She just couldn't tolerate the thought of losing this idea by throwing out her huge stacks of old magazines.

What eventually helped Andrea out of this spiral was defining clearly what she valued most, and having beautiful, harmonious surroundings were very high on her list. Working with values in psychotherapy involves not only identifying our values but also, crucially, considering which behaviours lead us closer to or further away from our valued way of being. Andrea slowly realized that accumulating magazines in order to capture that one perfect idea was in fact leading her away from, rather than towards, her ideal. She came to understand that, in her current situation, discarding rather than accumulating would be more likely to fulfil her wish to be surrounded by beauty.

Very slowly and gradually, and with much help and encouragement, Andrea was able to start letting go of her excess possessions, pausing frequently to appreciate how this liberated her home and allowed space for her beautiful objects to be seen to their best advantage. Of course, she also had to find a way of letting go of many of the objects she had accumulated. This was helped by an initial strict assessment of exactly how beautiful the object was! If it was less than exquisitely beautiful, it didn't make the grade and could be passed on. There were still many, many objects in the 'exquisitely beautiful' category, of course, but Andrea reflected on another of her strong values, which was to enhance other people's lives by sharing beauty with them (her artistic mission). She reflected on the joy another person would experience when they saw one of her objects in a charity shop and took it away to brighten a corner of their own home, and this helped ease the pain of releasing them.

It was a slow and careful process, and Andrea still has many, many beautiful objects, but she no longer accumulates magazines, and she finds it easier to be discerning when acquiring objects. She says that therapy has helped her understand that moving in a valued direction doesn't always feel easy and in fact often feels like a move towards pain, but ultimately aligning her behaviour with her strongest values leads to calmness and a sense of being contented with herself, something the contents of her shipping container could never provide.

Five hoarding hacks

Rather than providing five takeaways in this chapter, I thought it would be more useful to share the wonderful five hoarding hacks artwork developed by Heather Matuozzo and playwright and illustrator Stephen Jackson. Heather is the director of Clouds End, a community interest community specializing in supporting people with hoarding behaviours. Stephen is also a director of Clouds End.

From: *100 Hoarding Hacks* by Heather Matuozzo and Stephen Jackson

5

Organizing strategies

Being organized provides me with a sense of control and comfort as well as safety. Control knowing where my passport lives, comfort knowing I have back-up supplies of toilet rolls and deodorant, and safety knowing I have control and comfort!

Being organized, without the obsessive need to have perfectly folded fitted sheets and herbs sorted alphabetically provides us with a sense of control of our thoughts and feelings. I know many people who clean, tidy and reorganize their under-the-stairs cupboards, handbags, linen cupboards as a way of filing away the clutter in their heads.

Some people thrive on organized chaos. Some people feel uncomfortable in environments that are too stark, tidy and clinical. I know when I am being creative with writing or my artwork there is generally mess and chaos around me and this actually helps with my creativity. It's about what suits you, how you thrive and what your lifestyle is. It's also about being able to not feel stressed by day-to-day living with the hurdles of disorganization. Studies show that being able to focus on tasks is made more difficult when our senses are overloaded and overstimulated. Outer organization contributes to inner organization.

Here are some strategies that you might want to use and that I have found to work well with the many people I have helped in the ten years of organizing homes.

The art of the to-do list

To-do lists are critical in achieving what needs to be done. I write a list every night so my head isn't whirling with worry about what I need to get done the next day. Lists help us declutter our minds. Lists can be 'will do' lists, 'want' lists or 'wish' lists. Our lists need to include self-care nourishing activities. Include days in your week when you do not have a to-do list. Once I was listening to comedian and writer Jenny Eclair on the radio and she came up with the phrase 'listless days' – not languid days but referring to days when we do not write a list. Sundays are my listless days, and on these days I go with the flow and actually it can feel quite liberating knowing that I am having time off for me – task-free.

The 'to-do' list versus the 'ta-da' list

There will be days when you may not be able to achieve what you set out to do and with that can come feelings of failure and defeat. The 'ta-da' list is an antidote to the 'to-do' list. Rather than look at what you have not yet done, you can look at your 'ta-da' list which includes everything you have done that day – from making your bed and brushing your teeth, to putting items in the dishwasher.

We are not perfect and we are human, so incorporate both kinds of list and it will help you realize just how much you can or cannot accomplish in a day and provide an improved, more realistic sense of what can be achieved and help with better planning of day-to-day tasks. On days that life might feel challenging it's much better to focus on the 'have done' rather than on the 'still to do'.

Our to-do lists can include mundane things like 'pay parking fine' or 'buy olive oil', but try to also include your hopes, affirmations and dreams as well ('meet a new friend', 'write a poem', 'spend time playing with the kids'). My to-do list as I write this book is to include writing on one subject each day. If a to-do list reminds you of to-dos that never happened, find another name such as 'My Monday', 'My schedule', 'Stuff to do'. Whatever you call it, a to-do list will act as a compass and helps you plan for the future.

Analogue or digital?

I am an analogue girl in a digital world so I love my brightly coloured, lined sticky notes for my daily to-do lists (barring Sunday). I know others who prefer digital. It's about having one system rather than multiple ones and about what works for you. Sometimes when I am out and about, not necessarily clutching my to-do list, and something comes into my mind about a book I want to read, something to research or remembering an action I need to take or an item to purchase, I will use my phone to email myself and then transfer what is in the email to my to-do list.

Ticking off or crossing off and prioritizing

I love to cross things off my to-do list whereas I know some prefer to give the task a tick – there is something very positive about this (perhaps a memory of our schooldays). Also, I number the priorities on my lists whereas you might prefer to put a star or a circle against what is an essential or a must. I also prioritize tasks that I know need mental energy to complete, so that I work on those tasks when I'm at my most productive.

The body double

In the world of ADHD coaching, the term 'body double' was first coined in 1996 by Linda Anderson who is a pioneer in the field. The body double's role is to keep the person on track and help reduce any likely distractions, help provide focus and clarity. Having someone with you 'holding space' can create a sense of accountability and help you finish tasks you find challenging, tedious, difficult or uncomfortable.

Body doubling can be effective for anyone, not just for those with ADHD. The presence and connection with another person can provide the dopamine needed to 'get things done'.

When I work with people in their houses, when they are dealing with difficult paperwork like filling in a tax return or passport form, I see my role as a quiet, calm person that sits alongside them. I act as their blinkers, too. I have come to realize that if I start talking about mundane topics this can act as a distraction, so I sit on my hands and that in itself is what is needed.

It doesn't need to be a physical presence, an online presence is also very effective and I use this to get some of my accounts down. I co-work remotely via Zoom with Amanda (mentioned earlier) and get loads done this way.

It's not about providing solutions or doing it for them, but just being there in their presence. Choose your body double with care.

My keys, my phone

These are the most frequently lost items – there has even been a rap song (by Mr Zip) about losing keys and phones. Wallets, too, can often be mislaid. Finding homes for items that are logical to you is important. For example, find a secure place in your hall to keep your car and house keys (not so close to the door that they are visible and reachable). Find key rings for your keys so you can identify what key is to be used for what purpose. So many people move from one home to the next with so many keys that they no longer have any idea what each is for, but they worry about letting any of them go.

Phones, too, easily go on walkabout – I have a bright orange cover on mine so I can easily locate it or you could use an online tracker.

Are you a plonker?

I go into so many homes where there are piles of letters dotted all around the house, or random parcels and shopping bags dumped down willy-nilly after a client has returned home. I think it's important that we can chuckle to ourselves about our habits and behaviours, so I often say to my clients: 'Are you a bit of a plonker?' Practise putting things away rather than putting them down.

Command centre

Identify places for everything coming into your home. Ask yourself: 'Where is this item going to live?' Introduce landing strips for items. Also look at action areas – rooms where appropriate tasks get done. I use my study to action paperwork. I use my living room to read. I zone my areas for different tasks. Sometimes, if I am stuck, I change direction and use a different room for a task or even just turn my chair around to see things from a different perspective.

Be transparent

Many of my clients forget where things are, so the use of clear cupboards, taking doors off wardrobes, using clear storage boxes and transparent plastic folders can aid with retrieving items. Visual aids are a great asset towards being more organized. Glass jars, glass cabinets ... anything that prevents the frustration of not remembering where things are or even if you have them in the first place!

Calculate the chore time

As we saw in Chapter 4, time perception can be very challenging. There are certain chores and commitments that determine our time, and to help take control of time it can be beneficial to list all the steps needed to complete a task, along with timings.

An example of this might be doing the weekly shop: How long does it take to drive to the supermarket? To go up and down the aisles? To go through the checkout? And then drive home again and put everything away (remember, straight away!)? Break down all of the sequences needed to complete the task but also understand what the task involves. Asking someone to do the shopping may be too literal – what does 'doing the shopping' mean for them? What does it involve?

Wriggle room

I am always on time for dinners or parties, meetings, appointments and events and in fact it makes me feel quite stressed if I know I am going to be late. I think this goes back to my childhood and my father's intolerance for unpunctuality! I have, however, learned to manage my anxiety about lateness, and mindfulness has certainly helped with this.

Allow buffer time in between tasks and in your schedule. Sometimes I arrive a quarter of an hour early for a client so I can breathe, plan, schedule and prepare for the session ahead. Block time out for you to be, rather than to do. Be a human being and not always a human doing.

The school run

Many of you will relate to the morning stress of the school run. I had three children to get to three different schools and then had to get myself to work on time as well. It was a military operation. To eliminate as much stress and anxiety not only for me but for the kids, I did as much the night before as possible and tried to make sure everyone had told me what they needed for the next day's school – violins, rugby kit, swimming kit, donations for Harvest Festival – and whether it was a non-uniform day, there was a school trip, or even if it was an Inset (in-service training) day. Most of the time we got to the three different schools on time, without stress, and I then in turn got to work on time – and I would give myself a high-five, and considered this to be the biggest achievement of my day. This might not, however, be the case for many parents.

Sarah's lateness

I worked with Sarah on and off for many months with the organization of her home, her paperwork and garage, but invariably our sessions would start off with Sarah being in a low mood and often in tears as she had not been able to get her son to school on time. The school kept a register, and after so many mornings in a row of her son being late, she was called in to talk about why. She felt shame and embarrassment as if she had failed as a parent.

We looked at all the steps we could take to ensure her son was on time for school and this involved calculating how long each action took and breaking it down to the minute. We worked out the time taken for her child (with her help or not) to:

- brush his teeth
- wash his face
- comb his hair
- put his uniform on
- use the toilet
- have breakfast
- have his bag packed with homework and items needed for the day (e.g. violin)
- prepare his packed lunch
- put his shoes on
- walk to school/take the bus.

We also added in some contingency time.

Sarah took stock of the steps she needed to put in place, which included accepting that her challenges of managing time was a challenge in her executive functioning. Once she stopped berating herself, she found confidence in asking for help from her husband to take her son to school on some days, her son became more independent with the tasks needed to get out the door, and Sarah used alarm reminders on her phone as prompts for managing time. There is now so much less stress in the home for everyone, and Sarah is feeling so much better about herself.

Be mindful of not overcommitting, of what is stealing our focus, what is eating into our time, if we are nourished, if we have had enough rest and sleep, what our schedule is, what our plans and priorities are – and always include time to just be.

There are various tools we can use to help us manage time effectively, build up routines, structures and plans for the day and look at who might be able to help lighten the load. Tools I recommend include:

- analogue clocks
- online calendar
- family timetable on a notice board
- timer.

There is a wealth of books on time management (see Resources and further reading) to help us – it's a case of finding strategies and flexing the muscle to apply them.

Time chunking

Time chunking, or time boxing as it is also commonly known, is a great way of allotting time for tasks that might need doing where they are similar in the action required – researching a plumber, completing a tax return, cleaning the oven/fridge. This allows time to be put in to manage our environment and have dedicated time rather than wait until a long weekend or, to use that frequently flourished phrase, 'When I get round to it'. 'When' does not define time!

Time chunking allows us to factor time in for tedious tasks as well as more challenging ones, and it means we can allocate time for both knowing when you are feeling more energetic and focused and allocating other tasks for when you are not at your peak.

It is also a great way of ensuring we are also factoring in our time for self-care, exercise, reading, meditation, time out – whatever form relaxation might take for you. It also allows us time for looking at the internet, scrolling and clicking through TikTok or YouTube videos. We are containing time and giving ourselves licence to pursue these activities without feeling guilty that we are wasting it.

Time chunking allows us to help provide the right balance of work, relationships and personal life and stay true to what our core values are.

I am steaming off wallpaper in my living room at present. I am planning on having it replastered in August. I am scheduling times on the weekends – Saturday and Sunday mornings for an hour each – to steam the wallpaper off. This way, I'm hoping I won't be bored to tears, and it keeps the momentum up. When I am feeling cold, rather than put the heating on, I actually get up and do some steaming.

James Wallman, the best-selling author of *Stuffocation*, has written another book, *Time and How to Spend It: The 7 Rules for Richer and Happier Days*. The seven observations he makes are, in summary:

- We have more leisure time than ever, but it doesn't feel like that
- We don't feel like we have much more leisure time because we are misspending it
- We're misspending it because our society has placed high value on work and a low value on leisure
- Because of this, we've been trained how to work but haven't been trained how to live
- Knowing how to live has become more difficult, and more important today:
- Because of the internet and our always-on, always-there devices
- Because there are more things than ever to do in today's experience economy.

Misspending our time is like winning the lottery but only taking some of the winnings.

If we learn how to spend our leisure time, we can use our time better, and access previously untapped reserves of happiness.

Decluttering tips

I found hundreds of books on decluttering when I searched the internet, and that's not to mention the plethora of podcasts, websites and TV programmes offering tips!

Marie Kondo, the author of the best-selling *The Life-Changing Magic of Tidying*, which has sold over 5 million copies, has been recognized by *Time* magazine as one of the 100 most influential people in the world. The Konmari (Marie Kondo's nickname) method is to declutter and sort stuff by categories and encourages people to hold party-like blitzing sessions of their possessions. She is quite ruthless and even suggests putting your toaster away each night as well as emptying your handbag. Many of my clients love the method she uses of rolling clothes, and I agree that it can be very satisfying to open a drawer of folded, rolled and organized clothes.

Tidying can become its own mania and curse. Kondo herself has recently recognized, after the birth of her third child, that she cannot always stay on top of the mess her children create and has herself 'let go' of the need to tidy. She would rather spend time with her children rather than tidying up after them!

I know that clutter is not just physical; it can be emotional and mental and clutter can actually contribute to the inner turmoil we already feel. Our homes are often a reflection of our minds. More and more books are looking at the wellbeing of our minds and how to calm the chatter and clutter that can often rage within them.

Each object that comes into our home should command our attention. We need to understand its value for today, its connection with our past and if it serves our future.

Keep it simple

Simple questions and clear snappy sayings can help the decision-making process with regard to possessions. Here are some simple yet affirmative prompts and quotations:

- Remember the 3Cs – chuck, cherish, charity
- Use the principle 'One in, one out'
- Everything in its place, and a place for everything
- Would I replace it if it went?
- Would I miss it?
- When was the last time I used it?
- Does it enhance my life in any way?
- How many do I have?
- Is it broken?
- Is it out of date?
- What is the worst thing that could happen if I let it go?
- Anything that evokes negative thoughts can be disposed of. Why be reminded of bad times?
- If in doubt, chuck it out
- Is it a stranger, an acquaintance or a friend?

The OHIO rule

OHIO is an abbreviation for 'Only Handle It Once'. This rule is very effective in the workplace as a time management tool – for example when dealing with emails. The same rule can also be applied to decluttering homes and saves time on decision making and possible avoidance tactics: 'I'll think about it later', and so on. The concept is to pick up an item and then decide at once:

- Does it stay? If so, decide where it should live.
- Should it be recycled? Then put it in the recycling bin.
- Should it go to charity? Put it in the charity bag.
- Should it be thrown away? Put it in the rubbish bin, or put it outside to go to the recycling unit.

Identify an area in your home as a processing area to sort through your belongings. Once you have made a decision as to the destiny of an item, ensure it leaves the house in a timely fashion as this not only prevents any wobbles in your decision-making abilities but also brings refreshed energy into your home.

The above list is one that you can select from and add to. If the options above feel too drastic or cut and dried, then maybe consider the next option.

The 'keep for a week' rule

A client we regularly worked with devised this rule. His life was busy and fulfilled, and he found joy and excitement in new technology. Although committed to the decluttering process, he quite often needed time to think about whether he could let go of any item and set it aside for a week to decide on its fate.

Having a box or pile of 'doubtful' items takes the pressure off for some people. If there is an element of doubt over whether or not to let go of an item or to keep it, it is best not to pressurize yourself but to create a 'dilemma pile' and keep it for a period of time – a week is about right, I think. This should allow you time to process the item and to decide whether or not you want to keep it.

However, do be mindful of the fact that, while you are sorting, the dilemma pile should not be the biggest one. If it is beginning to look like it is, then it might be worth delving into why you are hesitating so much about reaching a decision. I advise my clients to put brightly coloured sticky notes on the items that are to 'keep for a week'.

Grouping and categories

It is important to simplify clutter-clearing sessions. Sorting through just one area of a room ensures that you are not overwhelmed with having to process many categories of items, and means that the decision-making process is much easier. Another way to conduct a session is by grouping items together. This really helps; it makes the decision-making process much easier when items are brought together in one place. It is far easier to process your clutter if you are only reviewing one category of it rather than having to deal with a mish-mash of different items.

You might want to decide that you are tackling clothes first, or paperwork, or your collection of dolls that is scattered all over the house. If this feels too overwhelming, break the process down even further – for example, instead of tackling all your paperwork, focus on one aspect of it. Once you have established that you are reviewing, say, magazines, bringing all the magazines together from around the home will enable you to get a realistic handle on the volume and make decisions more quickly.

Establishing rules

Clutter is essentially delayed decision making, so to empower and help yourself when decluttering makes the process that much less challenging. Remain focused on one area, and recognize when you are flagging and take a break. Some people set a timer for 15 or 20 minutes and review their progress at the end of that time.

We have found that the establishment of certain rules will usually make sessions less challenging. Rules help break down the decision-making process even further and provide clear criteria for decisions, which in turn will help prevent you feeling overwhelmed.

For example, many of my clients have vast amounts of clothes and can't begin to decide which ones to keep. So, when reviewing clothes, a simple rule would be that the ones that no longer fit go out. For one male client, the rule was that, if a pair of trousers had a 42-inch waist or below, they were deemed too small and could therefore go to charity.

Another rule could be to do with how long objects have been in the house. In the same client's case, we applied the rule to magazines over two years old and so recycled any over this age.

Other rules that may be helpful to you include the following:

- Out-of-date food is to go
- Newspapers that are more than x years old are to be recycled
- Magazines that are more than x years old are to be recycled
- Food containers with no lids are to be recycled
- Out-of-date medicines to go back to the pharmacy to be safely destroyed

- Chipped or broken crockery (because it can be dangerous and cause infections) is to be recycled
- Junk mail is to go in the recycling bin
- Old shopping catalogues are to be recycled – keep only the most up-to-date Argos catalogue, for example, and dispose of the older versions
- Put out any clothes that don't fit.

You might also want to apply a rule to get rid of the following:

- broken appliances
- unused toiletries
- unwanted presents
- old receipts – date to be identified
- old bills
- old to-do lists
- old shopping lists
- old Christmas cards
- shoes with holes in.

Label, label, label

Who doesn't like a label or a picture to know where things ought to live. We are taught this from the early days of nursery – a label for where your coat should be hung, your lunchbox put away, a label for the Lego crate, and one for the crayon container.

In my home, our recycling bins have labels on them. Airing cupboard shelves could have labels on them – this one for towels, that one for sheets. Even remote controls could be labelled. Every organizer I know loves a label machine.

Five takeaways

If you're decluttering your home:

1 Establish simple rules and keep to them.
2 Stop when you feel overwhelmed and walk away for a while.
3 Tidy up after yourself as much as possible – put old magazines in a recycling bag and have them ready by the door to take out.
4 Celebrate the space you have cleared – buy some flowers for it, or enjoy using it again (reading in a cleared armchair, having supper at a table you haven't seen in years).
5 Reward yourself for what you've achieved – though not by buying any more stuff!

6

Procrastination and chronic disorganization

Procrastination is the tendency to repeatedly put off an important activity and focus on less important, easier ones instead, as a way of distracting oneself. We all put things off, but procrastination can become a habit, and one that is difficult to break. It can be seen as a form of self-harm and, if chronic, can lead to extreme stress, have an impact on relationships, our mental and physical health, and our career.

Understanding procrastination

Knowing why we procrastinate can often help us with accepting the barriers to getting things done. We all procrastinate for various reasons, and there are many causes for this. Essentially, though, we hate discomfort and hate the unknown, or anything that we do not feel confident about, and anything we might find tedious or uninteresting.

Procrastination is not about laziness or issues with time management. It can be an emotional regulation problem and is connected to guilt, shame and fear. On the other hand, some of us are perfectionists and will stall on a task for fear of not doing it perfectly (see Chapter 2). Unrelenting high standards can paralyse us into a state of inertia of not achieving anything and fear of failure.

A friend of mine, Lou, who is a teacher, often notices that her students procrastinate to the point of self-sabotage and leave things until it's impossible to take action or when action can have only partially successful results. She has noticed that once we develop this habit it becomes almost permissible to then not do things, because in the past we have tried and failed. She tries to work with her students so that they recognize that procrastination is not an excuse but a challenge, and therefore awareness can bring about change through reframing. So, if they (and we) recognize that they have the propensity to procrastinate but do not have to give in to the habit, they (and we) can do something.

Gaining a higher level of self-efficacy, a belief in our ability to do something, can help with procrastination, but so can the recognition that actually we would all rather go out to play than do tasks that feel like work.

Some thrive on a deadline, cramming things in at the last minute and finding that the external pressures and demands are helpful. The energy put into putting things off often takes away from the energy we need to complete a task, effectively reducing our available time. There is a saying: 'Procrastination is the thief of time.'

Let's identify our mindsets, our blocks and barriers and push through with a sense of peace and pace, and not punish ourselves.

Self-awareness, curiosity and self-compassion can help us manage procrastination.

Types of procrastinators

Identifying what type of procrastinator you are can help understand your blocks and barriers and adjust your mindset. My friend Janey Holliday, a life coach, has identified various types of procrastinator:

Chronic procrastinators

Short-term mood repair becomes a priority over everything else. They avoid doing anything remotely difficult and seek quick-fix, mood-boosting gratifications instead.

Sabotage procrastinators

These unconsciously avoid or delay something because, without them realizing it, it's taking them to a place their core beliefs aren't comfortable with.

Positive procrastinators

Those who underestimate the time it takes to do things, or make decisions to do things when in a good place, only to find they don't feel the same when it comes to the action needed!

'I can do it all' procrastinators

They want to do things, and have the will, skill, strength and belief they can do it. Only they can't because there's a mismatch of task, time and energy, and they don't like to admit they can't! So, they keep intending to complete tasks, but always have to delay or push them aside as, deep down, they feel they may not succeed.

Priority procrastinators

Overloaded with day-to-day life and time poor, priority procrastinators have to triage on a daily basis and so things always get put away to another day (this is 100 per cent me!). It is a clever form of procrastination in many ways, as priority procrastination can be a very good thing. But if this means that you never get round to those tasks at the bottom of your list, then it can ultimately lead to trouble – these things need addressing after all, otherwise they wouldn't be on the list.

Convincer procrastinators

These are the ones who convince themselves to avoid doing something by telling themselves that they 'absolutely will do it tomorrow'. And when they say this and instantly get a big feel-good hit from it – guess what? – they repeat the delay!

Distracted procrastinators

In distracted procrastinators, even though they may have clear goals and intentions, the 'bright shiny object' syndrome takes over. It could be interruptions from others, or distracting thoughts, or Instagram rabbit holes! They get (or rather allow themselves to be) pulled away because there are so many better things to be doing, other than what really needs doing!

Dopamine-deficient procrastinators

These procrastinators are on an unconscious quest for a dopamine hit. And while doing what they need will give them that, it's not now. They need it quicker!

Neurodiverse procrastinators

These are people whose brains really struggle with what neuro-typicals find effortless. They tend to have executive dysfunction, often have demand avoidance, and are more likely to be distracted. They can also have sensory influences or overload, too, which can impact planning, motivation and task completion.

Burned-out procrastinators

These are the ones who perhaps used to be motivated to do certain things but have nothing in the tank any more. They often 'try' using the old 'go, go, go, do, do, do!' tactic. But it doesn't work any more. They're not the only ones burned out – their motivation methods are, too. They usually beat themselves up a lot, and often don't realize that a change of circumstance or energy is the reason they can't do something. So, they hate themselves *even* more! But all that's required to help them is a different perspective and an adjusted mindset.

Rebellious procrastinators

These are people who rebel against what they need to do in order to be different or to rebel against those around them. They like to go against the grain; they're the mavericks of the world and they like to be doing things their way and on their terms. They often resist doing very useful but 'normal' things, or things that critical, righteous family members want or expect them to do.

Planning procrastinators

These are the ones who put all their energy into planning and have nothing left for the action. They're often stationery addicts – with plenty of folders and highlighter pens – who look really organized to those around them. But they're not! They look busy and can be busy, but often not with the right things. They can often suffer from impostor syndrome, too.

Micro-procrastinators

Throughout their day and week, just by doing the odd minute of something here, something there, micro-procrastinators think they are working towards their goal, not realizing that they could actually achieve it much more easily if they set apart a proper amount of time to get through it. These micro-procrastination acts can often take them down rabbit holes, so often they don't realize what's happening until it's too late. But the justification of 'just a little bit here and there' becomes their permission to continue this way.

'Lastminute.com' procrastinators

These convince themselves that getting things done at the last minute is the best policy. But this isn't actually true (it's actually a subconscious win-win to avoid failure while also being able to claim success, depending on the outcome – clever, hey?!). And this actually drives them to repeat the pattern.

Overthinking procrastinators

These procrastinators' thoughts are out of control. They make mountains out of molehills. They catastrophize and complicate everything. They can't switch off. They think more than they act, talk more than they do. And they overanalyse everything, which creates overwhelm and shut down.

All-or-nothing procrastinators

Or perfectionism procrastinators. There is a huge link between procrastination, perfectionism and rejection. As a child you may have taught yourself to aim for mega-high standards to avoid rejection from a loved one, forming the belief that 'When I'm perfect, I'm loved and accepted' (or something to that effect). But as an adult, these standards are too much and not attainable. So, we procrastinate doing them as we predict we will probably fail and don't want to be rejected. We create so much pressure for ourselves, while at the same time setting ourselves up for failure. Can you imagine how exhausting this must be?

Solo procrastinators

A lot of people living by themselves struggle to do things by themselves especially if they are neurodivergent and they do not have someone around them to help. This is a very common one.

Remember, a lot of people are a combination of, or possibly even all, of these!

Did you know?

Akrasia is the state of acting against your better judgement. It is when you do one thing, even though you know you should do something else.

Procrastination is 90 per cent mindset, 10 per cent action

Fuschia Sirois is a professor of psychology at the University of Durham, UK, and a world-leading authority on procrastination. She mentions that there is a lot of advice on procrastination which she claims is not always helpful. Addressing it is not about being stoic and showing self-discipline, she says, but understanding ourselves and not beating ourselves up about it.

Procrastination has never been a good thing despite some researchers arguing the benefits of 'positive procrastination'. In an article in *The Guardian* newspaper, Sirois says: 'Embedded in the definition of procrastination is that you unnecessarily and voluntarily delay an important intended task despite knowing that the consequences are harmful. How can that be positive?' Sirois goes on to point out: 'Procrastination is at its core an irrational and emotional act and a form of emotion regulation where sufferers avoid a task that might spark negative emotions, by disengaging with it or putting it off. Procrastination is a way of managing our emotions and by putting the task aside we get an immediate sense of relief.'[1]

[1] Mark Brown, '"There is hope": expert writes guide to tackling procrastination', *The Guardian*, 4 August 2022, https://www.theguardian.com/science/2022/aug/04/procrastination-expert-guide-book-advice-fuschia-sirois#:~:text=Sirois%20said%3A%20"Embedded%20in%20the,and%20emotional%20act%2C%20Sirois%20said

Famous procrastinators

Victor Hugo agreed to write his famous novel *The Hunchback of Notre-Dame* in 1829. The deadline passed for the delivery of the book and he was given a new deadline. Hugo came up with a plan in which he locked away all his clothes leaving himself with only a shawl to wear (so he wouldn't go out). He finished the manuscript two weeks early!

Leonardo da Vinci famously left many artworks unfinished as apparently he had difficulty focusing. His most famous art work, the *Mona Lisa*, took 16 years to complete. One of his patrons had to threaten Leonardo with bankruptcy to encourage him to finish work he had been commissioned to do.

Despite having written many captivating novels, **Margaret Atwood** is said to suffer from serious bouts of procrastination. Over the course of her 50-year career, she has had 18 novels, 18 poetry collections, 11 non-fiction books and 8 children's books published, among many articles and shorter works. But, according to Atwood, her success is down to something incredibly simple. In the morning, she procrastinates for a few hours, and by the time she sits down to work at 3 p.m., she is finally able to focus.

Five takeaways

1 Procrastination can be seen as a form of self-harm.
2 Knowing why we procrastinate can often help us with accepting the barriers to getting things done.
3 There are many tribes of procrastinator – try to work out which one(s) you belong to.
4 Procrastination is never a good thing – there is no such thing as 'positive procrastination'.
5 Break your procrastination habit and replace it with a positive one.

7

Core beliefs and making changes

For this chapter I'm going to start by handing over the baton to author and coach Amanda Peet. Amanda is, along with me, one of the founding directors of the community interest company Hoarding Disorders UK. She is also the author of *Mind Your Mind: Using the Power of Words* and also runs the wonderful YouTube channel Mind Your Mind.

What are core beliefs?

Core beliefs are like little vows that you make to yourself or that you agree with when someone else tells you. You can also inherit core beliefs and take others' beliefs on as yours. Here are some examples that you may be familiar with ...

A vow you make to yourself: A relationship breaks down because the other person wasn't honest with you. 'I will never trust anyone again' is a common core belief that is taken on after this situation. This can stick until you change that core belief or until another life experience proves to you otherwise.

Someone else tells you: You are at school and a teacher says, 'You are useless at maths/French etc.' Or perhaps you are trying to do something and it's taking you an age and your parent snatches whatever it is away and completes the task because they can't be waiting around for you. You may believe them and keep that core belief: 'I am useless.'

It doesn't matter what the task is: if your subconscious mind has collected that core belief, it will remind you that you are useless whenever you try to do something. That can be quite exhausting, and it stops you from moving forwards in life.

You inherit a core belief. It can become a family thing: you can inherit this information through your DNA, or you take it on as yours through family beliefs. Have you heard yourself or others say something like this? 'I will always be fat because being fat runs in my family.' The person who says this has a belief that, because their parents and grandparents are overweight, they will be too. How about this family belief? 'None of our family go to university, so there's no point in my trying.' Until these beliefs are challenged, they remain stuck in a family's belief system.

By changing these core beliefs, you can start to see improvements through all areas of your life.

When we make a decision or a choice, start an action or have a reaction, that information comes from two places. Five per cent comes from our conscious mind. Many of us believe that we are consciously making all our decisions. However, 95 per cent of the information comes from our subconscious mind. Our subconscious mind is like our super hard drive. It knows every single millisecond of every single day we have ever lived, and if you haven't decluttered in there recently, it can start to slow you down and drain your energy, robbing you of clarity and peace of mind. There is just too much going on.

If you have a core belief of 'I am not organized', every action, reaction or decision you take is completely backed up by that belief. Even if you try to get organized, your hard drive sends you the message, 'Don't bother, you're not organized anyway', and so you may feel like every time you try to get sorted you fail. Which can lead to another core belief ... 'I always fail.'

Checking in on your core belief health is very easy to do. You say the core belief out loud and find out if it feels true, false, or somewhere in between. I developed *Mind Your Mind* to help people do this for themselves and when they find a true negative core belief, they know exactly what to do. Saying them out loud is an important part of the process. When you say them in your head you can easily con yourself that it doesn't apply to you. Saying it out loud you can feel its intensity and how true it is for you. It can be surprising when you say some of them out loud and find them to be true. Give it a go: When you find them and release them without judging yourself, it can be liberating!

But how do core beliefs affect you day to day? Surely what I do is just who I am and part of my personality? That is partly true, but we are driven and guided by what we have in our subconscious mind. Here's an example.

Where is that form? Arrgghhhh!

Where is it? It must be in your bag. I left it here. Well, it isn't here now. Well, where is it? Look behind the sofa? Has it slipped behind a cushion? You had it in the kitchen. I put it with the washing. Why did you do that? There was nowhere else to put it. Where's the dog?

These and hundreds more are just of the questions that can go through our minds or that we speak out loud to ourselves, our partners, family, or even our pets. For some people who are struggling with being chronically disorganized this can happen more than once a day or you may feel like it constantly.

When things don't have their rightful home or an area where they can go until you can deal with them, things go missing. There are lots of core beliefs that can come with this type of disorganization.

If that form was for a child's school trip that is happening today, then here is a little look at just some of the core beliefs and emotions where that situation could raise:

- 'I always get it wrong.'
- 'I am a bad parent.'
- 'I can't look after my kids.'
- 'They are going to hate me.'
- 'I lose everything.'
- 'I am disorganized.'

Not to mention emotions such as guilt, worry, shame, embarrassment and feelings of failure.

These core beliefs will then continually run through your mind even when you are not looking for a school trip form.

If you live alone and that form was for your prescription, here are some of the core beliefs and emotions that may run in your subconscious mind from not being able to find that form:

- 'I can't look after myself.'
- 'I am just so embarrassed.'
- 'I can't ever get better.'
- 'I just want to give up.'
- 'I can't do anything.'
- 'People always judge me.'

This can result in you feeling even more tired and ill, as the core beliefs above back up your actions, reactions and decisions.

When you have more than just your lovely self in your home, it is important that not only are you organized but also that your family can learn those skills. I don't mean in a way that you will then become obsessed and that is all that will matter to you, more in a way that lets you live, love and laugh alongside the chores. The chores become small in your day-to-day living rather than feeling like they are the only thing in your life. Here is an example of the core beliefs that can be running around for you:

- 'I am not heard.'
- 'I have to do everything around here.'
- 'They treat me like a slave.'
- 'I have no energy.'

Add to this their buddies from the world of emotions such as anger, annoyance or frustration.

If you want to make a difference to the quality of your life, investigating and changing your core beliefs can be a great place to start, alongside changing your behaviours. They can take minutes to change yet the power of those little sentences can give you so much freedom. You don't need willpower; you just instruct your subconscious mind and then hand it over. Your subconscious mind is so fast that it starts to do as you have asked it straight away and you begin to feel the benefits.

A good place to start is to look around your home. Walk yourself through your home from the front door with a notebook and pen. As you pass an area that annoys or niggles you in a negative way, first write down on the left side of the page what area of the home it is, then on the right-hand side of the same page list as many emotions as you can that you feel when you look at that area. Carry on through your home until you have a full list of the areas that need to be tackled along with a list of emotions. You will probably find that the same five or six emotions keep cropping up. Here is an example of a list of emotions from a client I worked with:

Area	Emotions
Front door, shoes everywhere	Angry
	Annoyed
	Frustrated
Stairs - stuff on the steps	Angry
	Annoyed
	Despair
	Frustrated

Bedroom, clean washing from everyone in a right state, not put away	*Despair*
	Annoyed
	Frustrated
	Guilt

This process can leave you with the feeling 'What's the use?', but it has also left you with a to-do list. Those emotions you have listed can be addressed and released, so that the areas in your home are less emotional for you and therefore easier to tackle.

In the above example, the client – working with a professional declutterer – was able to set herself the task of one area per week. Some weeks she didn't do anything on those areas, just because life was too busy. And do you know what? That's OK, life happens, and there is no need to beat yourself up about it or put unnecessary pressure on yourself. Other weeks, she was able to either sort an area or make a good start on it. Once the emotions were released, she found it easier to look at the areas with some clarity of what to do. Alongside the emotions she also cleared the core beliefs of:

- 'It's all my fault.'
- 'I can't forgive myself.'
- 'I always put pressure on myself.'

Working with a professional can make all the difference. We all have friends whose eyes light up and want to help, but there is the worry for the person being helped that it will be done at their friend's pace and in their friend's way. With a professional to help, you can be assured that it will be at *your* pace and you will be listened to so that the systems put in place in your home are the right ones for *you*. Doing this means that it works for you and your family, and this way is sustainable. Professional help for a short time is a great investment to help you get back on track.

If your budget is tight, there is lots of help available for a DIY approach. To clear your own emotions and core beliefs, you can visit my YouTube channel @Mind-Your-Mind for talk-along videos: https://www.youtube.com/watch?v=_I3NqwZbcWg

Shame

We all hate to fail, and in many cases, we avoid getting started on a task, project or venture through fear of failure and the feelings of self-criticism, unworthiness and uselessness. With that can come problems with not starting anything new or fear of starting a task ... and then the procrastination and paralysis step in. Shame is a shared common experience. Shame can be very destructive for motivation. We self-sabotage as a way of protecting ourselves from feelings of shame. There is a close connection between perfectionism and shame. Perfectionism hinders any hope of our moving forward when we are looking to improve our environment, and acts as another form of self-sabotage. 'I cannot do it perfectly so I will not even try and then I will not be judged or feel shame.'

Shame dissipates when it is shared in safe surroundings. The American sociologist Brené Brown has written widely on shame and she compares the 'I am' of shame – where the focus is on one's identity – with the 'I did' of guilt, which focuses on behaviour. She says that the less we talk about shame the more it can take a hold on us. If we reach out to others and share our shame, it loses its hold. 'Me too' are strong words, and I think that is where support groups really help. Empathy does not support shame – the strength of 'I know how you feel' is powerful.

I work with many people who experience shame, and it can present itself in many ways – hostility, being difficult, silence, defensiveness or perhaps complacency. These characteristics are put in place to protect us from shame, though, of course, these 'shields of shame' don't really work. What we really need is what Brown calls 'shame resilience'.

Brown has identified four basic components of shame resilience:

- recognizing shame and understanding its triggers
- practising critical awareness of the influences leading to shame
- reaching out to others
- naming shame when it occurs.

Rather than silencing, withdrawing from and avoiding the feelings of shame, the theory of shame resilience involves moving towards self-compassion, courage and connection and thereby moving away from shame, which involves fear, blame and disconnection.

Dr Kristin Neff is a psychologist and pioneer in the study of self-compassion whose research has shown how the practice of self-compassion can help us move away from shame. It is about being kind to ourselves, learning to be our own best friend. Neff has identified three elements of self-compassion:

- self-kindness rather than self-criticism and self-judgement
- recognition of our humanity rather than feelings of alienation and isolation
- mindfulness rather than suppression and denial.

Developing self-compassion as a habit can really provide support and encouragement when we are dealing with the challenges of day-to-day living. It helps with resilience and improves our mental and physical wellbeing. It helps us to stop beating ourselves up. By acknowledging our strengths and accepting our challenges with curiosity and kindness, we can appreciate ourselves and reach our goals.

Change

We can all experience fear of change – and that's why we love our comfort zones. No one likes uncertainly and many of us fear change because of the uncomfortable feelings connected with it. Change is difficult: with change comes a feeling of instability, a lack of control and, very likely, stress, so we avoid it.

Change will occur for all of us – as we leave home, go off to study, get married, get divorced, move house, change relationships, have children, acquire a pet, change jobs, change shape, even just change a room around. With any change also comes a sense of grief – for something that was and no longer is. Some people adapt to change better than others, and we need to understand that we all grieve differently and experience change uniquely.

Did you know?

Metathesiophobia is an intense fear of change. It is often linked with tropophobia, which is the fear of moving, and neophobia, which is the fear of the new. The origin of the word 'metathesio-phobia' comes from Greek *meta* meaning change and *phobos* meaning fear.

We may stay in a job we hate, or in a relationship that is not serving us, because we fear the alternative of not having a job, perhaps, or being single. We stay stuck. The same applies to any change of habits or situation. We avoid change because of the fear of the unknown and uncertainty.

The fear of change can stem from the way our brains are wired, from overprotective parenting, views that have been formed, previous trauma, deprivation, insecure attachments and childhood experiences. The fear of change results from both nature and nurture.

If we want things to be different, that involves change. It takes courage and commitment to move towards our wanted outcomes and look at our mindset to do so.

Change talk

We often talk about a person's readiness for change, and the reasons for not making those change are complex. In wanting change, the first step is realizing you have a problem, wanting to make a change and acknowledging that you may need help to do so. Asking for help is sometimes the hardest part of getting started, as is knowing what helps looks like. For us to let go and look at our environment differently, we need to reframe dysfunctional thoughts and beliefs around our habitats and possessions and learn to tolerate uncomfortable feelings and emotions around our belongings. Developing good habits, learning to reframe our thoughts and holding a vision of what we would like our space to look like can go a long way.

The Prochaska spiral of change

Change typically happens in stages. There are many different models of change, but we will focus on the Prochaska spiral, properly referred to as the Transtheoretical Model of Behaviour Change, created by the psychologist James O. Prochaska. This 'readiness to change' model is talked about frequently in the organizing/decluttering and hoarding world, as there are similarities with how people manage smoking, eating and drinking. Our relationship with the organization of our homes and our possessions can ride the same wave, and sometimes there is low tide or high tide.

Here are some of the stages:

Precontemplation/getting ready

This is the stage of not thinking about change, not seeing that things are a problem, where people may be defiant and defensive. We often talk in the hoarding world about people not being ready. Often they say that there is nothing wrong. They quite often do not have an understanding about the implications and impact of their hoarding behaviours. There is resistance, and denial, too. People with chronic disorganization and hoarding behaviours will often change the subject and blame their environments on others.

Contemplation/being ready

Contemplation is a stage where people are aware that change needs to happen. At this stage ambivalence is often present as the person weighs up the pros and cons – 'I could do something today but maybe I'll start tomorrow.' Intentions are there, but there are no concrete plans. The person may be curious, wanting to understand more about their issues, but they may also be afraid of failure, looking for the perfect solution. This is the stage where ambivalence is often present.

Preparation

At the preparation stage there is a focus on the future and planning for change. This stage sees the start of setting small goals and the start of working out an action plan. There is a belief and willingness to change and an excitement at the prospect of a home being more organized and decluttered.

Action

Action is the stage of a person having worked on their organizational/decluttering issues. Clear and developed action plans have been established. It is at this stage that new habits are formed, commitment to change is strong, confidence is established and the positives are being felt.

Maintenance

Maintenance is the stage in which people are working to prevent relapse but they do not apply change processes as frequently as when they are in the action stage. They are less tempted to relapse and increasingly more confident that they can continue with change.

Relapse

Relapse is an unofficial stage of change often mentioned, but I prefer not to refer to it as such, as why would we embrace change in the knowledge that there will be a relapse? I think we should accept from the outset that we are going to have blow-outs and blips along the way and that is OK. It's to be expected. We can rebuild and reset. When my clients feel disheartened, I reaffirm the fact that we are not actually back at the beginning and that the resets do not take as long as the initial process or are as difficult.

The learnings we have when we need to reset any part of our lives further strengthen our resolve and commitment.

Tips for overcoming fear of change

- Draw on your support system – whether friends, family or professionals
- Flip the script and recognize and manage those negative thoughts
- Let go of perfectionism
- Know your 'why'
- Know what the worst-case scenario is

- Breathe and ground yourself in the now
- Be aware of the 'what ifs?'
- Devise a plan B
- Draw on your previous achievements and successes
- Train your brain to embrace change
- Create a vision
- Look into your future
- Recognize that sometimes things might feel worse before they get better
- Put positive rewards in place.

Learning styles

It is important to recognize how you learn, how things stick and how you remember things, but it is also important for anyone helping you to know too. You may have heard of the idea that we all respond best to different styles of learning. That is exactly what the theory of the seven learning styles supported. All of the styles capture an individual strength that likely helps a person retain information more effectively. They each focus on one of the five senses or involve a social aspect. This theory is – or rather was – popular because, by finding an individual learner's style and tailoring teaching to it, it was thought their efficiency could be improved. The seven styles of the theory are:

- visual
- kinaesthetic
- aural
- verbal
- social
- solitary
- logical.

However, more recent studies have debunked this theory as an effective way of teaching and highlighted it as a so-called 'neuro-myth'. A group of experts in the field of educational psychology wrote to the UK newspaper *The Guardian* to say, 'Such neuro-myths create a false impression of individuals' abilities, leading to expectations and excuses that are detrimental to learning in general, which is a cost in the long term.'[1] In other words, attempting to put learners into boxes and trying to only give them material that matches their 'style' isn't going to make them retain information any better. Most people benefit from a range of teaching techniques, and utilizing different learning methods can actually improve learners' adaptability.

Nevertheless, it's certainly true that there are a variety of learning methods people respond to. Have a look through each one, and ask yourself: Do you find them all equally engaging? Is there one (or more) that you prefer above the others? Maybe you have your own learning techniques that aren't covered by any of the learning styles.

- **Visual** Visual or spatial learners supposedly retain information best by viewing pictures or images and respond well to colours and mind maps. These logos represent the main aspect of each learning style. Do you like to learn by remembering symbols and images?
- **Kinaesthetic** According to the theory, kinaesthetic learners are all about doing things physically. Role playing, using things like flashcards or carrying out the action physically can help them learn things better.
- **Aural** Aural or auditory-musical learners should retain the most information after hearing it.
- **Verbal** Verbal, or linguistic, learners are supposed to respond well to written or spoken words, using tools like rhymes and acronyms.
- **Social** Social, or interpersonal, learners are meant to work best when they participate in study activities with other people such as quizzing each other or having a study group.
- **Solitary** Solitary, or intrapersonal, learners supposedly work best alone. Making notes and reciting them back are useful activities when studying by yourself. Most of us will have to do some solitary revision at some point in our lives.
- **Logical** Logical, or mathematical, learners use logic and structures in order to learn effectively.

---

[1] Bruce Hood et al., 'No evidence to back idea of learning styles', letter to the editor, *The Guardian*, 12 March 2017, https://www.theguardian.com/education/2017/mar/12/no-evidence-to-back-idea-of-learning-styles

Five takeaways

1 Investigate your negative core beliefs, say them out loud and then let them go.
2 Practise shame resilience – name the shame, share it with others and be kind to yourself.
3 As you embark on a process of change, be aware of which stage you are at: are you ready for change but still trying to work out a plan, are you setting yourself small goals or are you now an old hand, with changes bedded in?
4 Understand that, when you undertake any kind of change, there will be relapses and blips, but be kind to yourself – they may be inevitable but they are also temporary.
5 By embracing the learning style(s) that suit you, you can make changes more fluidly and easily.

8

Breaking habits, and making new and better ones

A habit is defined by the *Cambridge Dictionary* as 'Something that you do often and regularly, sometimes without knowing that you are doing it.' Making the changes we want in our lives isn't necessarily about willpower; it is about changing and forming our habits. Habits are what make our habitat. Organizing can become habit forming.

There are many theories on the frequency of how many times we need to do something for it to become a habit – that is, we are no longer especially aware of our doing it. There is a widespread belief that establishing a habit takes 21 days. Phillippa Lally, a research associate at University College London, has debunked this belief. She found through her research that the average was 66 days, with some people taking as many as 254 days and some only 18 days. She states: 'We modelled the habit-formation curve, where it goes up in the first place and at some point reaches a level where it's as habitual as it's going to be, then plateaus – so my message from that is it's very variable.'[1]

The trick, of course, is to persevere – however long it takes you to change a habit or establish a new one. In the following I'll share some techniques with you that have worked with my clients.

Doing it for ourselves

To reach a goal, we need to have aligned behaviour and positive habits. We need to have a goal that is specific to be able to harness a habit which in turn becomes a behaviour. Saying you want a tidy house is too broad and needs to be broken down into how

---

[1] Quoted in Emine Saner, 'Five ways to form a good habit that sticks', *The Guardian*, 4 August 2019.

we are going to do that. This then minimizes planning, decisions and willpower and becomes a behaviour that is more likely to stick if we know the positive outcomes our habits create and we enjoy the reward of our behaviour. We need to feel pleased with what we are achieving, for ourselves rather than for anyone else.

Linking of habits

Linking any activity with a habit you have already woven into your routine can make a new habit stick. So, for instance:

- You could put your rubbish in the rubbish bin on your way out to walk the dog
- After your cup of coffee you always wash up
- When you unlock the door, you put the key on the key hook
- After you do your food shopping, you put items away.

Another way of thinking about linking one habit with another is to think to yourself: 'While I am here …'

James Clear, author of *Atomic Habits*, writes about 'habit stacking', which is essentially what I have described.

Autopilot

Many of my clients will declare that they do not have any good habits like regularly washing up, filing or making their bed. So I ask whether there are habits that are not necessarily 'ought to' habits but happy habits like listening to the BBC Radio 4 soap *The Archers* or starting the day with a coffee or walking the dog. Cultivating healthy and happy habits and acknowledging that our habits will sustain us is key to thinking about embracing change.

Our habits become something we are not aware we are doing – from brushing our hair, to setting our alarm, to flushing the loo and, for some of us, making our bed. Repetition builds habits, confidence, dexterity and speed, and there is a potential for us to change any tasks that we now consider arduous and time consuming into something done automatically, without thought, without discomfort and without distress. Habits protect us from overthinking. We do not need to think; the decision has already been made.

Our subconscious mind loves to sit in the comfort zone of familiarity, and by default our brain likes to stay on cruise control/autopilot as there is a sense of predictability and sameness. Any change can feel like a threat and with that comes a resistance to change. Research by Wendy Wood shows that 43 per cent of what we do every day is performed out of habit.

A 'safe harbour of habits'

Having a safe harbour of habits, as long as they are healthy habits, can sustain us during challenging times. The breaking of a habit can be just as hard as making one, so in a way we can rely on habits just being there whatever situation we have to face. We may be grieving or unhappy, but our good habits safely anchored in our mind and body will help see us through.

Making our actions and our behaviours automatic is what makes us reach our goals. It is not about self-control or willpower. Success is about relying on habits, not willpower. Let's not be mean to ourselves. Organize your habits to reflect your values and what is important to you.

My relationship with the gym

A few years ago I decided I needed to lose weight after gaining quite a few pounds when I started to work from home, build my own business up and re-establish a new routine. I enlisted the help of a personal trainer and was introduced to the gym. Gyms intimidate me; I don't necessarily enjoy exercising in public or the loud music that apparently helps drive you to keep going on the dreaded treadmill. I know, however, that I never regret a session at the gym and it is now part of my routine. I am not motivated to go, but actually it is now so automatic that I put my leggings and trainers on first thing on a Monday and off I go. The reward of going to the gym outweighs the decision not to. It is no longer a conscious decision – I don't even think about it. However, I do know that, if I didn't do it first thing, it just wouldn't happen.

A change of landscape

Our routines can be disrupted at times especially when there may be life changes such as moving house, starting a new job, retirement or starting a family. This may be the catalyst for new habits, and when this happens it is important to adapt our routines to accommodate our habits. We saw this in the COVID-19 pandemic which provided us with many opportunities to forge great new habits, abandon old ones, but also create unhealthy ones. We had endless days of repetition. Seize the opportunity of any life changes to create good habits.

One habit at a time

I would suggest you always allow the first good habit to become ingrained before embarking on a new one so as not to set yourself up for disappointment. You do not want to overcommit yourself to expectations that may be too hard to achieve, so start small.

You may have days when you are not in your typical routine, and it is worth noting that it doesn't actually take long to press the 'reset' button. 'Starting small' is always a good way of introducing a habit. Building a habit takes time, and it needs to be acknowledged that building a habit may often bring discomfort. Understand that, in the short term, it may be hard, but that it will eventually become so easy that you wonder how you ever found it so daunting.

Gluing of habits

To help habits stick, display visual cues around your home. For instance, if you are trying to learn a new language, then place your Italian dictionary next to your armchair. If you are trying to improve your health by taking additional vitamins, have them by the kettle so you establish a habit of taking them with your morning drink.

The power of sticky notes

While I was self-isolating during lockdown and feeling a range of emotions, I recognized that I needed to cultivate good habits and routines to manage my days at home. So each night I wrote a sticky note to remind myself of the things I wanted to do/needed to do and things that I knew would improve my wellbeing. For instance, my sticky note might include reminders to:

- *read*
- *exercise*
- *do jigsaw*
- *wash floor*
- *write book.*

Try creating sticky notes for habits you might want to create to help manage your home better:

- Put refuse bins out the night before
- Take washing out of the washing machine as soon as the cycle has finished
- Put away washed-up and dried items to maintain a clearer kitchen
- Put the house to bed before going bed. (There is nothing worse than waking up to the mess of the day before – best to start the day with today rather than tackle yesterday's baggage!)
- Make the bed first thing
- Never leave the house without taking either the rubbish or recycling with you.

ABC – anchor, behaviour, celebration

This technique is referred to in B. J. Fogg's book *Tiny Habits*. As the title suggests, one of the author's key concepts is starting small and this applies to any kind of change we embark upon. Tiny is achievable; it is safe; it doesn't rely on motivation, willpower or self-control. The author breaks down the forming of habits into three tightly related baby steps:

- **A – Anchor** Introduce the new habit to an already existing habit. So, for instance, after brushing your teeth, floss them too. Or after you have made your bed, put your clothes away. An existing habit reminds you to do a new behaviour.

- **B – Behaviour** This is the new behaviour: after brushing your teeth, you floss them. This is done straight after brushing your teeth.
- **C – Celebration** The celebration of the behaviour is really important, but can be easily forgotten, so choose something that sits comfortably with you – a quiet 'well done', a punch in the air, self-applause by clapping your hands. Always celebrate straight after the new behaviour. Our brain is hardwired to seek out pleasure and taps into more of the positive experience of how success feels. It seeks more of the reward.

Repetition, routine and rhythm

The more we repeat a behaviour and the more we practise, the better we become – this might be learning to walk, driving a car or speaking in front of an audience. How did I learn to spell or remember my times tables? By repeating, repeating, repeating. The more we do something the more dexterous and confident we become, and the more that something will be woven into the routines and structure of our days.

Of course, routine can feel stifling to some people, and feel limiting, rigid and oppressive. They see routine as a drainer rather than a sustainer. Others resist the idea of routine because they may have failed at a routine in the past and do not want to feel that failure again, so do not even try. Routines can seem scary and restrictive; we crave spontaneity, so resist routine. The irony is that you can be more spontaneous within the framework of a routine because it builds in time for what matters. Once you've got the routine engrained in your daily life, you have more, not less, time for fun!

Routines help us get things done

Having a routine that fits in with our personality and our energy level, and one that is not too onerous, strict and limiting, is important. As is having a routine that can be tweaked and be flexible. As a child I remember we had a fixed weekly menu plan. It felt so confined – macaroni cheese on a Tuesday, steak on a Friday ... I hated it. To this day I like the spontaneity of not deciding what to eat until the morning, so to accommodate that I have a freezer with a choice of homemade meals. I think it's about achieving a balance, blending the routine and non-routine into every day.

We are born into a world of routine – as children we experience the daily round of getting up, having breakfast, getting to school on time, lessons, lunch, home time, homework time, bath time, teeth time, bedtime, sleep ... However, there is also playtime, and I think as adults we have forgotten about the joy of play and see it as an indulgence. Even after we have notionally grown up, we need to build playtime into our routines. We also need to have days of no routines to accommodate the stresses of our lives and the demands on our time. Laundry will never go away, to-do lists will never be complete, inboxes will never be empty. Allow listless days and bring forward days.

Donna's brick wall

Many of us may well resonate with Donna's struggles of managing a family, relationships, jobs and finances. She has to cope with the challenges of having four children, all with learning difficulties, as well as four cats and one dog, while also facing harassment from one of her neighbours. What's more, Donna has a diagnosis of OCD, autism, dyspraxia and ADHD and also has hoarding behaviours. Her diagnosis, combined with the challenges of being a mother, has meant that her environment – both her home and her car – is often disorganized and cluttered. When she is feeling fed up (which she often is, as each day is, she says, like waking up to a brick wall she has to try to tear down), she shops and shops for anything. Her shopping mainly involves toys for her children, toiletries and items related to significant events such as Christmas, Halloween and Easter. Donna admits that her shopping habits alleviate her feelings of stress and provide her with a dopamine hit that she then needs to seek more of.

As I write this book, I am still working with Donna. We have worked out that, if we can create new habits and provide external long-term support to help her maintain the home, her environment will change and she will feel better about herself. We also know that she will benefit from therapeutic input but this is not at present available.

One of Donna's main CD issues revolves around laundry. To store her stuff, she keeps three storage units, one of which is full of unwashed clothes. Some of the laundry has gone mouldy, some is a bit mucky because the cats have urinated on the clothes, and some are just dirty. The difficulty we have faced is the processing of her guilty thoughts that she has not been able to stay on top of her laundry, as well as the hyper-focus on what clothes represent what occasion, what clothes could be passed on and whether her house can even accommodate the returned clothes.

Our strategy at present is to have a local laundrette pick up two bags of laundry each week and return them the following week. This seems to be working so far, though we are mindful that there is then the hyperfocus on ensuring that she allocates the right laundry basket to the right child with socks matched up. She worries, too, that the baskets might get knocked over, and clothes trampled on. The cats see the laundry baskets as an ideal place to catnap.

She has given up drinking Coke which has been really helpful in terms of her ability to focus and reducing her anxiety. She has managed to have her cats chipped which means they can roam outside.

Slowly but surely Donna is adopting new habits, new strategies – but as ever it is a work in progress!

The baggy routine

This term was coined by Matt Haig, author of *The Book of Comfort*. 'Get a routine baggy enough to live in,' he tells us. Routines allow us to achieve what needs to be achieved on a day-to-day basis, but with the demands, pressures and challenges that everyday life throws at us, we need to adapt to these demands and not beat ourselves up that we have not achieved all we set out to do. Having a baggy routine allows us to be kind to ourselves, but also to still hold ourselves to account and adapt to the given situation. You could compare a baggy routine to a baggy pair of jogging trousers – sometimes that is just what we need, and it allows us to be flexible and adaptable while not being overcritical of ourselves if we prove not to be superhuman.

A baggy routine essentially supports us without restraining us and allows us to accommodate the unexpected, to down tools, to rest and digest when we need to, and to find joy in the art of being rather than doing.

We are not aiming for a pristine sterile environment which requires constant attention, time and energy but a home that functions to meet our needs and do the stuff that really matters to us. Some people need things fluffed up and not particularly ordered. I know that, when I am writing, I need to eliminate distractions but actually like a little chaos around me. I take comfort from Albert Einstein, whose desk and surroundings were often muddled and messy, as this helped with his creativity. There is a difference between disorganization and mess, and sometimes messiness creates the greatest work of art, the most beautiful poem, the best decisions.

Acquiring and decluttering of habits

Decluttering applies much to our minds as it does to our homes, and that includes our habits. Some of our habits, though once good or neutral, may have stagnated and no longer be good for us. For example, perhaps we no longer drink wine for pleasure, but out of a habit. We may stay in a relationship or job because it has become a habit, not because we love the person or are passionate about our work. We may keep our possessions just because they are there – another kind of habit.

Try to be conscious of your habits, even the most deeply ingrained ones, and ask yourself: Which habits are worth keeping, and which are now redundant and no longer serving me?

Five takeaways

1. Making the changes we want in our lives isn't necessarily about willpower; it is about changing and forming our habits.
2. Link new good habits with old, existing ones – what James Clear calls 'habit stacking'.
3. Allow a new good habit to become ingrained before embarking on a new one.
4. Don't underestimate the power of sticky notes as you try to entrench new habits.
5. After anchoring your new habit, remember to celebrate your achievement – your brain will seek out more of the same.

9
Helping others with chronic disorganization

Witnessing others – especially family members and close friends – as they struggle with chronic disorganization and the very real distress they go through can be distressing in its own right. For example, young children growing up in a CD or hoarded house not only have the challenge of living in a cluttered, chaotic environment but also face the pain of seeing a parent they love unable to cope with day-to-day living. Likewise, adults may see a parent, sibling or other relation – perhaps after a divorce, bereavement or other traumatic life event – struggle to adapt to their new reality, find their ability to organize impaired and/or develop hoarding habits.

How can we best help these people we love who are in such distress? As adults we may be tempted to rush in and organize people's lives and houses for them, but as Amanda Peet pointed out in her contribution in Chapter 7, this can sometimes exacerbate distress. People with CD issues need to make changes at their own pace and on their own terms, so that real change is achieved, not quick, temporary fixes. They need, too, to understand their own issues and motivations and thus be ready to embark on their own journey, not be rushed along to a destination that someone else has decided for them.

For this reason, if at all possible, it's best to call upon the help of a professional who can work alongside the person gradually and over time, in a dispassionate, respectful yet empathetic way. Sometimes therapeutic intervention may be required too. Of course, if the person's CD is putting them or others in immediate danger, then more drastic steps will need to be taken. Generally speaking, though, softly, softly is the way to go.

To begin this chapter, I will turn to Marie Bateson, who runs the *Cut the Clutter* website and blog and who here talks about how professionals use interpersonal intelligence with clients and owners of hoarded houses. Her words, garnered from many years' experience, have much to offer all of us when we are dealing with chronically disorganized people.

How can we use interpersonal intelligence with chronically disorganized clients? A professional's perspective

We need to be detectives when working with our clients. It is important that we understand how we are communicating with our clients and also that we understand what they are telling us, even when it is not verbally communicated.

First, we need to have an understanding of interpersonal intelligence.

Interpersonal intelligence is the ability to understand and interact effectively with others. It involves effective verbal and non-verbal communication, the ability to note distinctions between other people, sensitivity to the moods and temperaments of others, and the ability to entertain multiple perspectives. We will look at this on a simple level but there is a whole science behind this subject and lots of reading to dig down deeper.

Successful professional organizers generally have a high level of personal intelligence. Primal empathy is the ability to recognize the emotions of others, and people who are adept at this are aware of when it is and when it isn't appropriate to show an emotion. When we are body doubling with our CD clients we need this skill.

Communication is not just verbal. We communicate with our bodies, eyes, nose, hands and so on. Eye contact is cited as being the strongest form of communication by leading psychologists. The eyes show many emotions – fear, happiness, tiredness, exasperation, hatred, love, suspicion, anger, hurt, delight.

We must ensure that we make and keep eye contact with our CD clients. This keeps them calm and focused and they feel listened to. Remember that they will be anxious; you might be, too, but it is important to show no apprehension, just kindness and understanding.

Never look shocked at the situation as the client may be very ashamed and they might have taken a long time to seek help. The last thing we want to do is set them back.

We may claim to be non-judgemental but how do we convey this?

When we visit for the very first time how does the client see us? We must show sincerity and a genuine smile is necessary to put them at ease. The fear will be high, and we can encourage them to relax with words, but our body language has to mirror the words.

Do we ever roll our eyes or screw up our noses?! Do look out for eye communication in your client, too. We can see tiredness or even despair, and this needs to be managed. Maybe it is time to finish or time for a break. If they appear defeated by the process, make time to stop and discuss what they are finding overwhelming and what you can change.

Don't turn up your nose if there is an odour – try to ignore it. Clenched teeth when dealing with something unpleasant sends the signal that this is a bad situation. Try to inwardly shake it off and be unfazed. Our mood and emotions can trigger the same in others. If we are bored or tired, we mustn't show it. Never sigh when the client has slipped back into an old habit or makes a wrong choice.

When is it appropriate to use humour? Not usually on the first few visits till you get to know someone. You can usually sense when the time is right, and if you don't feel it then don't just try it out. Can you use touch? A small touch on the arm to encourage or when giving praise for a job well done is very effective. Harder to know when their personal boundaries come down, but it can be very powerful if it isn't used too often.

Always try to get them talking. It really doesn't matter if the first session is one of discovery as long as you are putting this person at ease and building their trust. You may well be with a CD person for some time, so do not be discouraged if they take time to give you any eye contact. It may be embarrassment. Keep using it yourself and it will happen organically.

Look for moments of clarity, light-bulb moments; they are really rewarding and easy to spot. Save them and use them in a positive manner as previous examples of when things were working – especially in moments of overwhelm.

The more experienced we get the easier it is to tune in and notice things about our client that isn't being said.

Remember the body does not lie!

Marie's opening statement about being a detective is for me especially meaningful, as I believe that 'understanding the meaning in the mess' is crucial for both the chronically disorganized person and anyone trying to help them. When I am asked to assess someone's home by a social worker, environmental health professional or housing officer, I always use my professional curiosity and walk back through a person's life with them. All our homes can at times become places that do not serve us, places that become storage units, places that become uninhabitable, messy, dirty and chaotic, but we need to uncover the causes and triggers that underline this. It can be as a result of depression, bereavement, self-neglect, lack of life skills, illness, hoarding, cognitive decline, urinary tract infection or executive dysfunction, to name but a few. Again, it's all about being a detective.

Dorothy's story

Dorothy first contacted professional organizer Donna in 2021 following a fall in which she had sustained a long-term injury. This fall likely occurred, Dorothy had explained, as a result of too much clutter on her stairway, which she attributed to her struggle to keep things organized owing in part to her autism spectrum disorder (ASD). This, on top of having recently been widowed at a young age, had left Dorothy feeling increasingly distressed, and she knew it was time to reach out for some support.

During my first visit with her Dorothy explained that her current mobility issues had meant that basic household tasks had overwhelmed her and that she needed to find a way to get on top of them that didn't involve friends and family members, who, although well-meaning, were too gung-ho, she felt, in their approach.

I could see why Dorothy felt overwhelmed: the whole of the downstairs of her home was awash with clutter and laundry. I noticed balls of wool, pieces of thread, half-finished craft projects, gaming remotes, a library of books in piles of varying heights and stability ... I moved a few pieces of paper saved for decoupage projects to reveal boxes that had been filled with pre-loved CDs and computer games, ready to be sent off to a service like Music Magpie, but not having quite yet made the transition out of the door. I noticed empty Amazon packaging, discarded after it had been excitedly ripped open to free the next bit of kit or craft material. There was no doubt that Dorothy had a thirst for creativity. This observation was confirmed in a later conversation with my client, who referred to her penchant for craft materials and computer games (and all the associated paraphernalia) as 'brain fuel'. Further exploration of this concept opened a fascinating conversation, which helped me better understand her tendency to accumulate 'stuff'.

Dorothy's ASD, coupled with her intellect and thirst for creativity, means that she finds it hard to 'stay still' mentally. She explained to me that 'doing nothing' is torturous to her and spoke of how a recent lull in her workload had left her reliant on her creative imagination to while away the hours until she could come home from work. With little outlet other than Amazon at her disposal, Dorothy explained that she would often end up using the online shopping platform to acquire the materials to realize the creative masterpieces that she has been conjuring up in her mind all day.

Over a period of two years we tried a few approaches, before finding what worked best for Dorothy. Meeting just a handful of times a year, it was important to maximize the effectiveness of the time we did spend together. To facilitate this, we found that me going in to do a 'blitz' while she was at work, a few days before we met, worked well. By 'blitz' I simply mean consolidating laundry into one place, ridding the house of any discarded packaging, making floor space, clearing space to sit on soft furnishings and some light cleaning of surfaces (e.g. in the kitchen). This reduced the feeling of overwhelm for Dorothy when we did meet, enabling her to focus on decluttering, categorizing (and organizing) and storing her belongings.

Dorothy's need for 'brain fuel' meant that we needed to put in place storage solutions for the multiple balls of wool, knitting and crochet needles, tapestry and cross-stitch thread and other paraphernalia, as well as for her gaming equipment. Fortunately, Dorothy possessed a large shelving unit (which took up one wall of her bedroom) with deep shelves, each with 'baskets' in the square spaces. We labelled each of these baskets with either a craft or gaming category and set about organizing her 'brain fuel' into their newly assigned homes. This storage solution has continued to serve Dorothy well.

Furthermore, Dorothy found herself psyched about the impact of clutter on mental health, and podcasts (e.g. one on hobby clutter) were very helpful in enabling her to reflect upon her need for 'stuff'. Indeed, as a result, she has cancelled subscriptions to games she no longer plays and sorted through hundreds of spools of thread, keeping only those she will need and donating those she won't to a craft charity. Dorothy noted that an unexpected upside of this exercise was finding things she's forgotten she had, enabling her to complete previously unfinished projects.

Of our work together – which will continue at Dorothy's chosen pace – she recently reflected: 'I feel as though, as time goes on, my mind is being combed out, a bit like untangling matted hair.' I don't think I could think of a better analogy if I tried, given that there have been several occasions during our work together when I have found myself untangling electric cords attached to all manner of gaming consoles, or unknotting spools of thread or bundles of wool!

Working with Dorothy, as I increasingly understood her need to keep her mind busy with creative thoughts, I was reminded of the joy of creativity and of the anticipation of completing a creative project. I was reminded in this moment, too, of Alain de Botton's book The Art of Travel *in which he muses over the notion that it is often the anticipation of the travel that brings one more joy than the trip itself. I mentioned this to Dorothy, and she said it really resonated. Interestingly, research on happiness cites creativity as having a positive effect on mental wellbeing, so it makes a great deal of sense that thinking (or anticipation) about creative projects is a great way for Dorothy to self-soothe. Creativity is something to encourage, not discourage. However, stemming the flow of the plethora of incoming hobby-related paraphernalia was still an important part of our work together – it just took time, and a great deal of trust. Which brings me on to the importance of our relationship.*

Working with a person in their own home, to help them unpick years of disorganization and clutter, means you are meeting that person not only at their most vulnerable, but in the intimate setting of their own home. There is no doubt that, much like counselling, professional organizing is relational work. Getting to know Dorothy over time, I learned what she was comfortable with and what she was not ready for. I learned when to use humour to disarm, and, conversely, when it was time to be serious. I learned, too, when to let silence be there, with no need to fill that silence with anything, but for her to know I was there. I learned when to gently challenge and, importantly, the skill of not colluding with her to validate choices that may not have been in her best interest. All these delicate moves require a strong foundation. A strong relationship.

Playfulness, acceptance, curiosity and empathy (PACE)

PACE yourself ... Born out of his work on attachment-focused family therapy, American psychologist Dan Hughes developed PACE, which stands for playfulness, acceptance, curiosity and empathy. This trauma-informed approach lends itself well to helping people with hoarding tendencies, many of whom have experienced trauma and adverse experiences. Furthermore, the acronym itself seems particularly apt given that it implies moving at a steady speed and taking things one step at a time – exactly the gentle approach that is required when helping people with hoarding tendencies.

So how can we implement PACE?

Let's begin with playfulness. Playfulness facilitates a level of exploration of emotional processes that may not be accessible through more direct approaches. People who hoard may experience a great deal of shame, which can impede even the best-intentioned offers of help. However, because shame and playfulness cannot coexist, the element of play can help break down the barriers that shame puts up. This can be explained by Stephen Porges's polyvagal theory. According to Porges, a professor of psychiatry at the Kinsey Institute, our tenth cranial nerve (the vagus nerve) has two pathways (dorsal and ventral). The dorsal vagal nerve responds to fear (including shame) and elicits a freeze response, while the ventral vagal nerve (also referred to as our social engagement system) can be activated (e.g. through playfulness) to bring us back to safety and stability (known as homeostasis).[1]

But what do we mean by playfulness? Presumably, playing 'catch' with a much-loved item isn't going to curry favour with our helpee. In the adult sense, play relates to curiosity. Over time, as we build trust with the person we are helping, an open playful approach can reassure them that there's no right and wrong way of approaching their clutter issue.

Furthermore, humour works well to stave off any feelings of shame, and given that that we know perfectionism can be a characteristic of a person with hoarding tendencies, providing them with that safe feeling that they can't mess up can really help open their willingness to explore.

When supporting a person with hoarding tendencies, playfulness can counter shame and over time can help them reach a place

---

[1] S. W. Porges, *The Pocket Guide to the Polyvagal Theory: The Transformative Power of Feeling Safe*. W. W. Norton & Co., 2017.

of acceptance. This is important, because when coming from a place of acceptance, everything is open to exploration. For example, feelings of self-loathing or despair can be accepted as transitory, as how things are in this moment.[2] By validating the feelings experienced by the person with hoarding tendencies, the helper enables them to accept themselves just as they are in the here and now, which can counter shame and the associated feelings of stuckness (freeze) that come along with it.

Curiosity can facilitate useful 'play'. When supporting an individual in exploring why it may be that they are anxious about letting go of a hoarded item, a helper, by remaining curious and asking such questions as 'What part of you is feeling that?', may help the person acknowledge that the item reminds them of a time in their childhood, which may elicit conversation about an unmet need that this item may be representing, or, conversely, a happy memory. Either way, the feelings attached to the object may need exploring and accepting before the person feels safe enough to let go of the item.

This curiosity is an important skill for the person with hoarding tendencies to adopt and apply on their own, too. As we know, for any intervention to be sustainable, the person experiencing challenges with hoarding needs to be onboard with their own recovery journey. If they can be curious and feel safe to roam around their minds, they may feel less afraid of what may come up for them. As helpers, we can facilitate this by applying empathy at every step of the way. Without empathy, curiosity may feel too intrusive, but by validating the feelings coming up for those we are helping, we can enable them to become more confident exploring their feelings about their beloved items, including when they feel ready to let go.[3]

---

[2] P. A. DeYoung, *Understanding and Treating Chronic Shame: Healing Right Brain Relational Trauma*. Routledge, 2021.

[3] 'Dorothy's story' and details on PACE reproduced here courtesy of Donna Bartlett, with thanks for her contribution.

Dos and don'ts

If you are helping someone else declutter:

Do ...

- Put yourself in the person's shoes – how would you want to be treated?
- Match the person's language – how do they refer to their possessions?
- Be guided by the person you are helping
- Show your humanity
- Establish trust
- Use humour
- Set and keep boundaries
- Exercise patience
- Use active listening skills
- Use positive language
- Defuse negative talk
- Have intermittent breaks
- Set a pace

Don't ...

- Use judgemental language
- Take over or talk down to them
- Force a system, suggestion or idea
- Be a sergeant major
- Fill in the silences – the person may be trying to process emotions they are feeling
- Try to distract them with chitchat
- Complicate sessions with too many different tasks
- Try to do too much at once.

Five takeaways

1 Never rush in and try to 'sort someone out' on your own terms, as this can heighten their anxiety and rarely provides a long-term solution.
2 Work in partnership with the person, respecting their needs, opinions and space.
3 Gently, gently, does it.
4 Use your detective skills to work out what is really going on in a cluttered or hoarded home – the 'mess always means something'.
5 If you or they can afford it, consider getting professional decluttering help.

10

Chronic disorganization in later life

Later life can trigger or exacerbate chronic disorganization. Not only may we have a lifetime's possessions and clutter gathered around us but we may find that both physical and/or cognitive decline makes us less able to organize those things and our lives. Research suggests that older people with ADHD may experience symptoms that overlap with those associated with ageing. Triggers such as illness or the loss of a spouse – may leave us facing chores and tasks that previously we left to our partner – as well as the more general disorientation that accompanies bereavement and grief. Hoarding behaviours may set in as a way of coping with depression or trauma or sometimes as a result of dementia.

The techniques and strategies discussed throughout this book apply, of course, just as much to older people as to any other demographic, even if there are more likely to be the complications of health conditions and other issues. However, in this short, final chapter, I will focus on how my own parents dealt with the organizational challenges they faced in later life. In many ways, they provide a positive example of how good planning and other strategies can help us through a potentially difficult phase of our life and help us defuse the threat of disorganization. Old age need not at all doom us to cluttered homes and feelings of overwhelm, nor, after their parents' deaths, adult children to the exhausting and often heartbreaking task of clearing the former family home.

My father's lists and my mother's operating manual

Both my parents were organized, though I think my mother may have learned a lot from my father who I sometimes think must have been born meticulous, methodical and mindful. Before she married she had been a secretary and this, too, gave her strong organizational skills. In some ways, she had to be organized:

147

because of my father's job as a civil engineer, we had many postings abroad, so we were constantly moving house and school. My mother even created an operating manual so that when she went on holiday, anyone staying to look after the house knew how things worked.

This organizational nous of both my parents continued into retirement, even when inevitably health issues cropped up. Once my mother needed to go into hospital for a routine operation which meant the Thursday supermarket shop would have to be undertaken by my father. In preparation, she gave him a list of essential items. After the trip – which I think overwhelmed him somewhat – he decided to create a printed list by aisle order. So, on entering the supermarket – Aisle A comprised fruit and vegetables – he devised the list to incorporate the regular items they typically purchased there – for example, potatoes, carrots and apples.

As with many couples who retire, my father suddenly became very interested in the management of the household, and this irritated my mother beyond belief as her life was dedicated to looking after him, her children and her home. My father was effectively encroaching on her domain, and I think she may well have felt undermined. However, his efforts were always impressive.

Dealing with death and life after bereavement

After my mother died, six weeks after her family found out she wasn't well, our family was struck by how well my mother had organized a 'tidy death', from ensuring that her wishes were acknowledged, to the special treasures dispersed to her loved ones. She had already prepared a list before we knew she was ill about 'who was going to get what'. She died of cancer and by the time this was diagnosed the only option was palliative care. She spoke to my sister and me about what she wanted to happen about her funeral, which made it that much easier for us to manage the rest of our family in terms of what they might have wanted versus what she wanted. That aside, my father took control of the ship and managed all the administration associated with her passing. He even asked if there was a *Debrett's Guide* to follow.

After my mother's death, my father reflected on how well my mother had managed all of the household chores but realized that he did not know exactly what they were and when and how often they needed doing – this included everything from servicing the aga and defrosting the freezer to arranging for a chimney sweep to come and the annual boiler check. All of these chores were in my mother's head. Her operating manual needed his input. He asked me one day if I knew why the tumble dryer wasn't working. When I looked, I realized that both the condenser container needed emptying and the fluff filter needed cleaning.

Being an engineer, my father hated not knowing how to operate items and so he expanded the operating manual to incorporate daily, weekly, monthly and yearly tasks. There were reminders about riddling the coal aga, putting out empty milk bottles, putting out the rubbish and recycling on the correct day, when to pay the paperman, when to check the fuel consumption, how often to water the plants, and so on. This meant that even when he went away, he felt assured that the house would be well maintained and fully functioning.

My father's example made me realize that we all need a household manual for managing our homes. Many of my clients are baffled as to why they can function perfectly well in their work environment, but their home environment is a completely different matter. This will be for all sorts of reasons such as how much we have in our vessel or how much bandwidth we have, but I think we could all benefit from having a clear job description and guidance on how to look after our home environment. My father was ahead of his time!

The post-mortem chore list

Following the angst and minefield my father experienced in the weeks and months after my mother's death – having to work out which authorities to inform, which banks and building societies to notify, how to cash in policies, what to do with her possessions – he decided he needed to create a post-mortem chore list for his own affairs for 'when it was his turn'.

It was the greatest gift he could give his children, especially as his dementia began to advance. My sister and I met with him one Sunday and went through every detail imaginable that needed to be covered. So much consideration and thought was taken to ensure that we could easily sort out probate, deal with the tax office and sell the house. He had hoarding behaviours so did not want to declutter as such before he died but he knew we would take care of this.

After his death probate was granted and the house was sold in just five months. That is impressive, as I know for many people death can bring lots of complications. Having a will and a post-mortem chore list in place made it so much easier. It meant we were able to execute his wishes with as much precision as he would have wanted.

My parents' later life was not always easy and they faced challenges like any other, but they took every precaution to make sure everything ran smoothly, in life as well as death. There is a book on death clearing which is essentially decluttering while you are alive so your kids and family do not have to deal with it when you die. The title of the book is *The Gentle Art of Swedish Death Cleaning* by Margareta Magnusson, and it really does have some really useful tips in there.

I wish my mum had read it before she died, as I had all her love letters to go through – no one is perfect, able to think of everything. Margareta's answer to this particular chestnut was to put all her love letters in a box labelled 'Please do not read. Please shred.' That's a simple, clear piece of communication. Communication is key when you are decluttering. We should very much talk not about getting rid of things, but regaining space and letting go.

Five takeaways

1 The reasons for chronic disorganization in older adults can be just as complicated as for everyone else – do not jump to conclusions and just put it down to ageing.

2 Keeping lists is a useful practice throughout adult life, but can be especially so when we are older.

3 A household manual can be a wonderful thing, especially after the death of a spouse. In a shared household no one does (or should do) everything, so suddenly having to keep a house by oneself can seem overwhelming.

4 As an older person, consider preparing a post-mortem chore list for your heirs – they will thank and love you for it.

5 Communication is key when you are decluttering, at whatever age and in whatever situation.

Resources and further reading

Hoarding websites

Hoarding Disorders UK
www.hoardingdisordersuk.org

Hoarding Support
Advice, support and forum run by Jasmine Harman
www.hoardingsupport.co.uk

Overcome Compulsive Hoarding with That Hoarder
Excellent podcasts on hoarding.
https://www.overcomecompulsivehoarding.co.uk/category/podcast/

Stuffology
Advice and guidance on hoarding provided by Jan Eppingstall who has a
doctorate in the area.
https://stuffology.com.au/

Other resources

National Autistic Society
https://www.autism.org.uk/

OCD Action
https://ocdaction.org.uk/

Professional declutterers and organizers

Association of Professional Declutterers and Organizers (APDO)
www.apdo.co.uk

Institute for Challenging Disorganization (ICD)
https://www.challengingdisorganization.org

Therapies

Don't forget that the NHS advises that your GP should be the first port of call.

To find counsellors or psychotherapists who deal with chronic disorganization and hoarding, visit:

www.counselling-directory.org.uk

Hoarding icebreaker form

This created by Cherry Rudge (from the professional decluttering business Rainbow Red) for people seeking help with their CD or hoarding to take to a professional to start a conversation around these issues.

https://hoardingicebreakerform.org/

Further reading

Brown, Brené, *Daring Greatly: How the Courage to Be Vulnerable Transforms the Way We Live, Love, Parent and Lead*, reprint edition. Avery, 2015.

Clear, James, *Atomic Habits: An Easy & Proven Way to Build Good Habits & Break Bad Ones*. Random House Business, 2018.

Curran, Thomas, *The Perfection Trap: The Power of Good Enough in a World That Always Wants More*. Penguin, 2024.

David, Susan, *Emotional Agility: Get Unstuck, Embrace Change and Thrive in Work and Life*. Penguin Life, 2016.

Dawson, Peg and Guare, Richard, *The Smart but Scattered Guide to Success*. Guilford Press, 2016.

Fogg, B. J., *Tiny Habits: The Small Changes That Change Everything*. Virgin Books, 2020.

Kolberg, Judith, *Conquering Chronic Disorganization*. Squall Press, 2007.

Kolberg, Judith and Nadeau, Kathleen, *ADD-Friendly Ways to Organize Your Life*, 2nd edition. Routledge, 2016.

Magnusson, Margareta, *The Gentle Art of Swedish Death Cleaning: How to Free Yourself and Your Family from a Lifetime of Clutter*. Canongate Books, 2017.

Neff, Kristen, *Self Compassion: The Proven Power of Being Kind to Yourself.* Yellow Kite, 2011.

Peet, Amanda, *Mind Your Mind: Using the Power of Words*. Amanda Peet Publishing, 2021.

Pink, Richard and Emer, Rozanne, *Dirty Laundry: Why Adults with ADHD are So Ashamed and What We Can Do to Help*. Square Peg, 2023.

Wallman, James, *Time and How to Spend It: The 7 Rules for Richer, Happier Days*. WH Allen, 2019.

Acknowledgements

I have to start by thanking my family – Juliette, Sam and Sasha – for all your lovely support. Thank you, too, to all the people my work brings me into contact with. I learn every day from you but also from the many people whose homes I visit and who also share their stories in the many emails I receive and the telephone calls I take. Everyone has a story to tell about how stuff, mess and muddle impact on their day-to-day lives.

I am always humbled by the many people who open up to me about how they feel about their homes. I feel privileged that their frankness and bravery have enabled me to write this book, just as it did with *Understanding Hoarding*. Thank you.

I also give much thanks to the experts and academics in the field whose invaluable work and insights I have used or quoted in this book: Donna Bartlett, Marie Bateson, Sarah Bickers, Paul Cooper, Janey Holliday, Heather Matuozzo, Amanda Peet, Sharon Morein, Cherry Rudge, Gill Cooper, Jane Scott, Esther W. and Kate Wren.

Index